Labors
of
Love

Published by:

Farfallina Press

MLG & Associates
Farfallina Press
66 Witherspoon Street, Suite 115
Princeton, NJ 08542
mgalastro@mlgpubgroup.com

Introductions & Editing by Bruce Arant
Cover & Interior Design by: Jill Abrahamsen
Interior photographs by: Victor Nieves

ISBN: 9780984550739

Library of Congress Control Number 201093616

http://www.laborsoflovebook.com

Note: While all the birth stories included in this book are real, the names of the people, hospitals and birthing centers, have been changed to protect the privacy of the respective parties.

Labors of Love

A Doula's Birth Stories

Penny Bussell Stansfield

Published by Farfallina Press

Acknowledgements

My doula career began in 1997 with the launch of Desert Doula Childbirth Services in Tucson, Arizona. I am grateful to my fellow founding members Karla Baranowski, Marian Douris, Lisa Kiser, Patti Reich and Suzanne McFarlin-Wolkin for their hard work, dedication and enthusiasm. Desert Doulas continues to thrive to this day and has served thousands of women in the Tucson area.

Thank you to my mentors and teachers in the field of massage therapy, including Mark Caffarel, Jan Schwartz, Shelley McGrew and Michele Kolakowski who showed me the power of compassionate, healing touch.

I could not be a doula without the support of my colleagues at Hillsborough Massage Therapy, Gary Verhoorn, Portia Resnick, Debby Teal, Stella Nieves and Kathy Borsuk who are always ready to step in and work with my massage clients when I need to rush off to a birth.

Thank you to my fellow New Jersey doulas Amy Wright Glenn, Stella Nieves and Kathy Borsuk who are my trusty back-up doulas and my sounding board.

Thank you to my wonderful children Johanna, Alastair and Kate who never complained if I missed an important event in their lives because I was at a birth. Their enthusiasm for my doula work has carried me through many a long night. I am grateful to them for the opportunities they gave me to discover my own strengths and weaknesses when bringing them into the world. A special thank you to my husband Rob who has supported my work in so many ways and listened patiently to my rants about the condition of maternal health and outdated hospital protocols. In particular, he has spent hundreds of hours in front of the computer on my behalf, compensating for my appalling lack of technical expertise.

I wish to express my sincere gratitude to all my clients and their families without whom these stories would not exist. Whether their story is included in this book or not, I feel privileged to have accompanied these women on their journey to motherhood. I have witnessed their joy, their pride, their challenges and their accomplishment in bringing new life into the world. Each birth I attend deepens my admiration for the strength of the human spirit in general and the awe-inspiring power of maternal love.

Dedication

This book is dedicated to my children Johanna, Alastair and Kate, who have taught me the transformative power of birth, and to my husband Rob, my very own personal doula.

Table of Contents

Table of Contents

SIBLING BIRTHS (continued)

THE STORY OF MY YOUNGEST DAUGHTER KATE'S BIRTH

GLOSSARY

Foreword

"*Labors of Love*" is a brilliant collection of stories about one of life's most common of miracles – birth! Every second, births are unfolding all around the world, and each of them is unique. What can this diversity of birth experiences teach us? "*Labors of Love*" not only gives us a glimpse into the spectrum of possibilities with birth, but also reminds us of the wisdom that comes with sharing stories about this most magnificent of human experiences.

Author Penny Bussell Stansfield has had the privilege of attending hundreds of births as a birth doula. Thanks to her clients' willingness to tell their birth stories through Penny's rich, yet down to earth writing style, we, the readers, can jump right into these splendid birth stories. I laughed, smiled and cried as I read them. Enjoy feeling the emotions that these stories evoke in you as you peruse each page.

Reading "*Labors of Love*" also reminds me of what birth can teach us – patience, caring, compassion, intuition, trust, love and openness to the mystery and magic of birth. As you read "*Labors of Love*," be curious about what you can learn about birth.

Whether you're preparing for your own birth or are dedicated to supporting women through this journey, "*Labors of Love*" is a wonderful way to open to the promise and potential of birth. Perhaps "*Labors of Love*" will also inspire us to create more sacred space to share our birth stories in the future.

Thank you Penny for giving voice to these stories with your love, grace, transparency and passion. Thank you also to the families who opened their hearts and ours with each of their stories.

Happy birthing!
Michele Kolakowski BA RMT CD(DONA) CIMI

Registered Massage Therapist, Certified Birth Doula (DONA), Certified Infant Massage Instructor Supervisor, Health Center of Integrated Therapies, Longmont United Hospital
Co-developer and Faculty, Cortiva Institute Maternity and Infant Massage Program
Colorado, USA

Introduction

Every birth is unique; every woman has her own story. My role as a doula, also known as a professional birth assistant, is to support a woman in her informed choices. I have been a witness to over 100 births, each one an adventure into the unknown. My clients' priorities have ranged from achieving a totally natural birth with no medical intervention, to women choosing an epidural for pain relief as early as possible in the labor. Regardless of women's priorities and ideals, the birth journey is always a mystery and things rarely turn out exactly as planned. So women who wanted no interventions have at times ended up with a cesarean birth, and women who wanted medical support have occasionally ended up with an intervention free birth. My role as a doula is to journey with the woman on this rollercoaster called labor, to acknowledge and validate her feelings at all times and to offer her continuous emotional and physical support.

For every client, I write a detailed birth story. This is my gift to them. For this book, I have chosen a selection that portrays the amazing variation the birthing experience can offer. While all identifying details have been removed or changed, each story is an accurate and detailed description of how the birth unfolded. There are no embellishments, no romanticizing, and no scare-mongering tactics, as is so often the case in the mainstream media's portrayal of birth. These stories show the wide range of normal birth. Normal labor can vary in time from a few contractions to a few days. Normal contractions can be perceived as painless or unbearable. I have chosen real life stories that portray the widest possible range of birth experiences. This book will show you just how varied "normal" can be. The stories are filled with the myriad emotions a woman feels during birth: elation, fear, self-doubt, empowerment, anger, relief, exhaustion and joy, to name but a few.

These stories portray the unpredictability of birth. You can have clear birth preferences, plenty of knowledge about labor and know exactly what you do and don't want and this is all good. But ultimately, labor is a journey into the unknown. The best laid plans can be thwarted by a baby who will not move into the optimal position, by hospital protocols that do not match your preferences, by emotional states that are not in sync with physiological changes and countless other factors that might change the course of labor. These stories highlight the unpredictability of birthing and will help women to accept the mystery of the birth journey as it unfolds in its own time and its own way.

Women who have not yet had children will obtain a realistic idea of how birth is experienced in a variety of ways and settings. Women who have had children will be able to relate to these stories, clarify pieces of their own stories and learn something that will help them in future births or at any births that they might have the privilege of attending.

It is known that women do not forget their birth experience and that the long-term psychological impact is huge. A positive birth experience can empower a woman for the rest of her life; a traumatic and negative experience can affect her self-esteem forever. Studies have shown, however, that a woman's satisfaction concerning her birth experience depends most of all on how she is treated by her support team and her sense of active participation in the decision-making. That is why I am a doula. I understand how pivotal the birth experience can be for a woman and I protect her birth memory by empowering her during the birth and by writing a birth story for her to treasure for the rest of her life. My wish is that this book will help many more women to understand the birth experience and to have realistic expectations about this unique and exciting adventure called birth.

Penny Bussell Stansfield

Births with no INTERVENTIONS

"It took a while for Samantha to actually believe that she had given birth to a little boy, but the proof was right there as she held him in her arms for the first time."

CALLUM'S BIRTH

It's always interesting to note how our perspectives change with experience. As new employees, new students and of course, new parents (or parents-to-be) we are often inclined to approach the "newness" of our relative situations with, "a fear of the unknown." Experience, however, bolsters our confidence and empowers us to take on previously daunting tasks with courage. This transformation in self-assurance is strikingly evident in women (and couples) who have birthed multiple times. For these veterans of labor, it typically comes down to knowing what has to be done and "getting on with it." Such was the case in Callum's birth.

For the past three weeks, Samantha had been having early labor contractions. These apparently unproductive sensations had disrupted sleep, not to mention innumerable day-to-day activities for this busy mother of two. (Not counting the one she was carrying.) Although they looked forward to having a new baby in their household, both she and her husband Tom were unnerved by this sporadic barrage of false alarms. Their need for peace of mind brought them to the decision that this baby needed to be nudged into the world on the due date – and not one moment beyond.

And so it was, that the three of us met at Middlesex County Community Hospital, at 7:00 am on Monday, March 12th. The plan was that Samantha should have her waters broken, thereby bringing labor on. There was a slight risk that labor would not kick in and other medications would have to be used. This seemed unlikely, however, seeing as Samantha was already 4 cm dilated and her baby was lying very low in the pelvis. Staged for birth, her body was causing her extreme discomfort.

Our nurse for the day was Jessica. She was sweet, gentle and very open to allowing Samantha complete autonomy in her birthing choices. We were fortunate to have been placed with such a "hands off" nurse, as some are more comfortable playing a controlling role, which would not have suited Samantha and Tom. While we settled in to Room 327, Jessica asked Samantha myriad questions, some of which seemed totally irrelevant, but she apologetically explained that it was hospital protocol.

At 8:00 am, Dr. Kira Senko arrived. Samantha was delighted that she was to be the doctor on call that day, as Dr. Senko was her preferred choice among the doctors in the Practice. She examined Samantha who was four to five centimeters dilated,

80% effaced and the baby at -1 station. To allow for the passage of the baby, the cervix has to efface to 100% and dilate to 10 cm and the baby has to move from -4 through 0 to +4 station. Then she broke the waters and Samantha knew that there was no turning back. She was monitored for half an hour and then allowed to get up and walk around. Unlike the previous times, labor did not immediately kick in or speed up once the waters were broken. This baby was determined to take his or her time. We walked the corridors for half an hour – a short, rather dull circuit, enlivened only by the moments spent gazing in at the nursery, admiring all the newborns. Contractions were a little more intense than earlier in the morning and coming about every seven minutes. Samantha, however, was still walking and talking through each contraction.

A student nurse named Stella, who was clearly thrilled to be in such a great learning environment, joined Jessica. With Jessica's experience as a nurse and Samantha's experience as a laboring woman, this student was going to have a rich opportunity to watch two seasoned experts! By 9:15 am, Samantha decided she wanted an enema in order to feel more comfortable and hopefully speed up labor. Jessica performed another exam and discovered she had not changed very much since 8:00 am. This news must have been disheartening for Samantha to hear, but she never seemed discouraged and was more determined than ever to get things moving along. At 9:40 am she used her enema and resumed lying over the birth ball on the bed while being monitored.

At 10:00 am Samantha's dad arrived, having gotten the older kids off to school. He waited patiently in the corridor for several hours while Samantha continued in labor with his grandchild. It was sweet how he would say a few kind words every time we walked past him. By 10:30 am contractions were becoming more intense and Jessica noted that Samantha was in active labor. They were also coming closer together, but despite the intensity Samantha insisted on walking the corridors, knowing that movement was really helping move the labor on. Samantha never seemed to harbor any fear or desire to hold back despite the growing intensity of the contractions.

Eleven o'clock came and went and Samantha returned to the bed for her monitoring stint, leaning over the birth ball and rocking rhythmically with each contraction. By now the pain was more intense. We placed a warm sock on Samantha's aching lower back and Tom and I took it in turns to hold the Hoku point, a strong, pain-relieving acupressure point, located between the webbing of the thumb and forefinger.

In addition to relieving pain, acupressure can also be used to stimulate labor, which I did by holding the Spleen 6 point – four finger widths up from the inside anklebone.

Fifteen minutes later, Samantha was allowed off the monitor so we hit the corridors again. The difference this time was that with every contraction, Samantha needed to lean against the wall and focus with all her might on what was going on inside her body. She was magnificent, never allowing anything to break her concentration as she breathed slowly and calmly, allowing the wave of the contraction to roar through her body.

At 11:30 am Dr Senko returned from surgery and checked Samantha who was now 7 cm dilated and 90% effaced. This was great progress, but Samantha was as determined as ever not to let things slow down. Within five minutes, she and Tom were walking the corridors again while I waited in her room, happy to give them some private time together. When she returned to the room she decided to try the rocking chair for the next monitoring session. Being seated in this position however, seemed to slow the interval between contractions back down to about five minutes. This was not conducive to Samantha's game plan, so she was very open to Jessica's suggestion that nipple stimulation might bring contractions closer together once more.

One o'clock found Samantha sitting on the birth ball, leaning against the bed for support and discreetly starting nipple stimulation, which releases oxytocin from the pituitary gland in the brain. Oxytocin is the hormone that causes uterine contractions. The effect was almost instantaneous and the intensity, duration and frequency of the contractions increased immediately. There followed the toughest hour of the labor for Samantha, which she handled fabulously well. With each contraction she would sway rhythmically from side to side on the ball and moan in a soft low monotone, eyes closed, in total concentration on the powerful sensations sweeping her body.

I held the Hoku point on her hand for every contraction and pressed as hard as I could. Whenever my thumb started to ache, I would look at Samantha and feel humbled that I could even *think* of complaining. It was such a minor unease compared to the overwhelming intensity of her contractions. Jessica sat quietly next to us and was awed by Samantha's courage and ability to work with her body. She later said she would have liked to have been able to film the birth, to show prospective parents what a natural birth looks like.

Just before 2:00 pm Jessica went to fetch Dr. Senko, as Samantha was beginning to feel a lot of pressure. Moving from birth ball to bed was really challenging, in that the baby was fast on the way. With her usual stalwart determination, Samantha made the transition despite overwhelming contractions. The doctor checked her and said that she was fully dilated and there was only a small anterior lip on the cervix, through which she could push the baby's head.

At 2:00 pm Samantha started pushing with each contraction in the seated position on the bed. This caused her excruciating back pain, so she opted to move onto all fours. Three pushes later and we could see the baby's head at 2:07 pm. Tom put his hand down and gently massaged the baby's head while we all waited for the next contraction. Finally, at 2:10 pm, Callum Joshua was delivered with the highest possible Apgars of 9 and 9 at birth. Tom cut the cord and took his son into his arms. Samantha and Tom were thrilled and dumbfounded, as almost everybody had told them to expect a girl! It took a while for Samantha to actually believe that she had given birth to a little boy, but the proof was right there as she held him in her arms for the first time. He was alert, calm and so happy to nuzzle up to his mother's breast as the doctor delivered the placenta and put in a couple of stitches to prevent Samantha from bleeding.

Samantha's dad soon came into the room to welcome his newest grandson and I tried to get as much of the happy scene on film as possible. Tom left to pick up the older kids from school and bring them back to meet their baby brother. Meanwhile, Callum was weighed, measured, checked out and bathed – none of which appealed to him as much as his previous half hour of blissful breastfeeding. He weighed 7 lbs 5½oz, and was 21 inches long. Within an hour, the family was united and relishing their first hours with the latest arrival to the Baden family.

Samantha, you are an incredible woman and your strength and courage never failed you during this beautiful labor. Thank you both for allowing me the honor of being with you during this incredible birth.

BILL'S BIRTH

Isn't it delightful when things "work out?" As a doula, I'm so happy for the expect-ant mothers (or couples) I work with, who, after months of anticipation are privi-leged to have the type of birthing experience they had always hoped for. Because each birth is unique unto itself, it is impossible to assume that every detail will go as "planned." Medical intervention is a prime example. Regardless of one's determination to have a totally natural birth, it is important to remain open to the possibility that intervention might become necessary. That said, it is truly wonder-ful to see the "hoped-for" births come to pass. Such was the case for Shelley and Tim, who had hoped for – then had the good fortune to experience – the natural birth of Bill.

Shelley's baby was nearly two weeks overdue and she had reluctantly agreed to go in for an induction on the morning of August 4th. We spoke for a long time on the afternoon of August 3rd, and it was clear that Shelley was not happy about the situation. She so much wanted to allow labor to start naturally and yet her time was fast running out. She decided to have a nice, final evening with Tim rather than going in to hospital to have her waters broken and stay there. So they went out to eat and then went on to visit with her brother. Back at the apartment, she had a nice relaxing bath and went to bed. Within a very short time of Tim falling asleep at around 11:30 pm, contractions finally started. The power of mind over body is truly incredible. Shelley was desperate to avoid induction and here at the thirteenth hour, her body kicked into labor – just in time to save her from the pitocin induction! Her contractions came fairly close together right from the beginning. By 2:30 am, she and Tim were getting ready to go to the hospital, with her contractions occurring at about three minutes apart.

We simultaneously arrived at the hospital at about 3:10 am. Shelley's contractions were coming thick and fast, but she was coping very well and promptly refused the use of a wheelchair to get her up to the fourth floor. As we settled into Room 440, Tim made a second journey to the car to fetch all the paraphernalia.

Although Shelley's contractions were fairly close together, her behavior hinted that she was really in very early labor – chatting between contractions, making jokes and gen-erally being very cheerful. Our nurse for the night, Renee, was quiet and unassuming, although I was a little taken aback when the first thing she explained to Shelley was the procedure for epidurals. We all knew that this was something Shelley wished to avoid.

Renee hooked Shelley up to the monitors for thirty minutes to get a baseline reading for the baby's heartbeat and her contractions. She gave her an internal examination at 4:20 am and found that Shelley was 3 cm dilated and 80% effaced. I think Shelley was somewhat disappointed at this news, as she had been very much the same the previous afternoon. No doubt, she had been hoping that a few hours of contractions would have gotten her farther along. I was quick to point out, however, that the baby was moving down, and that this was an excellent sign. Moving the baby is part of the work that contractions have to do. Although she was disappointed, Shelley never allowed herself to become despondent, especially with Tim always there to encourage her.

By now, contractions were coming every two minutes and Shelley remained very active in order to keep things going. She walked almost constantly. We even went outside at one point to see if we could spot a shooting star or two from the Perseid meteor shower. We didn't, but it was good to move around. She also spent quite a lot of time on the yellow birthing ball, gently swaying and rocking to the contractions.

Tim was very attentive the whole time and was constantly giving gentle words of encouragement and love. Rarely have I seen a partner so totally involved and committed to the labor process as Tim – despite feeling nauseous *much* of the time and tired *all* of the time! He was 100% there for Shelley, and I was pleased to be able to go out and fetch him drinks and snacks. I could see that he never wanted to leave her side for one moment. We repeatedly played her lovely Pachelbel CD, to which she had so often relaxed at home. As the soothing strains of *Canon in D* swept about the room, she visualized relaxing during her labor. We also played my French CD "*Relaxation Psychomusicale*" which Shelley liked. She seemed to respond very strongly to music, and what with the dim lights and the soft melodies, we managed to create a harmonious and pleasant atmosphere even though it was a hospital room.

At 6:30 am Shelley was examined again and had reached 4 cm dilation. This was slow but steady progress. Shelley decided to get into the bath before Karen, the midwife, arrived to break her waters. Shelley agreed that breaking the waters was the least invasive way of pushing her into active labor – and given that she was two weeks overdue, the hospital staff was keen to "get the show on the road." Once the waters had been broken, she would no longer be allowed to get into the bath.

She got into the soothing, warm water at 6:45 am and remained in there with Tim until 7:10 am. This helped to relax her, just as the contractions were getting harder to work with. Shelley still kept moving after the bath; wandering around the room; hanging onto Tim during a contraction; sitting on the birth ball; doing some pelvic rocking and working brilliantly with the ever strengthening contractions. Tim's support continued to be unerring. He was *so* lovingly attentive and their cooperative intimacy was a joy to behold. Our day nurse, Linda, had arrived by now. We were all very pleased to discover that she was very supportive and respectful of Shelley's wishes. Linda was clearly very excited to be working with Shelley, as it was no longer common to have a woman in her care who desired a completely natural birth.

Karen finally arrived at 8:50 am and gave Shelley an internal examination. To our great delight, Karen announced that Shelley was now at 7 to 8 cm dilation – incredible progress in such a short time, especially for a first baby. This rapid progress was due to Shelley's ability to work *with*, rather than *against* the sensations of the contractions. Equally important, was Tim's loving support and her determination to "keep moving on." She never once struck me as being afraid, despite the fact she was going through a completely new and challenging experience.

Shelley was moving into transition and still coping brilliantly. Interestingly, she developed a couple of rituals such as jiggling her right leg and shaking her head backwards and forwards during each contraction. She was intensely in touch with her body, allowing the powerful sensations to flow through her and do their work. All this time, Tim was sitting on the birth ball next to the bed, utterly absorbed in Shelley's efforts and giving her verbal encouragement during each contraction. Between contractions, he would stroke Shelley and rub her back to try and make her as comfortable as possible.

At 9:30 am Shelley was clearly in transition. She was working *so* hard and still coped beautifully with amazing focus and control. The contractions were overwhelming but she never lost her nerve. Not once did I have to "take charge" and pull her back from the brink of panic, which typically happens during the transition phase. By 9:50

am, when she had to get up to go to the bathroom, the contractions were coming *really* close together.

At 10:00 am Karen examined Shelley again and she was at 9 cm. The cervix, however, was no longer changing because there was an anterior lip that was preventing full dilation. Karen tried to push the lip back over the baby's head during a contraction, but it would not stay there. Forty-five minutes later Shelley tried sitting on the toilet to get rid of the lip. This position can be effective in putting lots of pressure onto the cervix, from the baby's head. As we waited outside the bathroom, we could hear Shelley yelling "I don't like this." (That must have been putting it pretty mildly!) By now, Shelley had started to have the urge to push, but it was not going to be very effective until she was totally dilated and had gotten rid of the anterior lip. This gradually happened over the next thirty minutes with the help of several position changes. By 11:00 am Shelley was beginning to push her baby out.

It must have seemed like an eternity to Shelley – she had not slept all night and had been working so hard for many long hours – but in fact, her pushing stage was relatively fast for a first baby. She brought him down slowly but surely. Tim encouraged her through every contraction and must have counted to ten at least a hundred times, in order to focus her pushing efforts! For someone who had been fearful of feeling queasy during all this, he was doing heroically well. I kept thinking that he might pass out or throw up, but he never wavered in his task. Tim worked in total cooperation with Shelley, holding her so tight – it was almost as if *he* was pushing the baby out.

We could see the baby's head for nearly thirty minutes before he was born. This is not unusual for such a large baby and Karen showed wonderful patience in allowing him to take his time. She once mentioned that an episiotomy would bring him out quicker, but there was no medical necessity to do that, so we just waited a little longer. Each contraction was becoming more and more exhausting for Shelley and at times, she seemed to be at her wit's end – especially when there were unhelpful comments from Tina, the pediatric nurse. But she kept going and found the strength to birth her baby totally naturally, without any medical intervention whatsoever.

Bill Jason Hobbs was born at 12:12 pm on Tuesday August 4th, Shelley's twenty-seventh birthday. He weighed 10 lbs and was 22 inches long. Shelley did not have an episiotomy, only a small tear that needed a few stitches. The fact that Shelley birthed this beautiful big baby completely naturally is a tribute to her innate power as a woman. She demonstrated the ability of women to birth their babies without medical intervention when they have confidence in themselves and are surrounded by loving, patient and respectful companions and care providers. It was just what she and Tim had hoped for.

"Miriam was determined, however, to birth her baby despite her weakening contractions and growing exhaustion."

ANTHONY'S BIRTH

Perseverance – it is among the most revered attributes of the human spirit. Just look back across history. Who are the ones we've placed upon the pedestals? Who are our heroes? More often than not, they are those who never gave up, who believed in their cause and had the resolve to "stay with it," no matter what. In compiling this collection of birthing stories, my intent was not to write a history book – at least, not in the strictest sense. But these pages are filled with histori-cal accounts of real-life heroes – women who entered the uncharted territories of childbirth and persevered to the end, despite the hardships – heroes like Miriam.

At 5:30 am on Friday morning June 22nd, Miriam awoke to find evidence that her waters had perhaps broken. Contractions were brief and sporadic so she decided to wait until her scheduled 1:30 pm midwife's appointment and see what the day would hold for her. She and Simon met with Janet their midwife, who, after examination, announced that she was 2 cm dilated. Janet also explained that it was her mucous plug that had come away, and in fact, her waters were still intact. This was good news, in that it didn't put any pressure on how quickly the baby should arrive. (Once the waters have broken, the baby is generally born within about twenty-four hours to minimize the risk of uterine infection.) So Miriam returned home and took a nap. Throughout the rest of that afternoon and evening she continued to have irregu-lar contractions. Simon meticulously timed them, but the pace never consistently quickened. She worked with the contractions, trying a variety of different positions in order to find one that was the most comfortable. Unfortunately, she did not get much real sleep that night, being woken up every 10 minutes or so by a contraction.

The next morning continued in the same vein for several hours. But by late morning, contractions were beginning to get a little stronger and closer together. Miriam was beginning to realize that "this was it!" She called me around noon and asked me to come over. She wanted me to spend some time with her at home, helping her to work through the contractions as she felt like "she was losing it." This temporary and very natural bout of self-doubt only lasted a short while.

Indeed, by the time I arrived at 1:00 pm she was once again coping well with the ever-increasing intensity of the contractions. I found her lying on her side on the sofa, focusing well during a contraction and chatting merrily between them. (Incredibly, she remained cheerful for the next twelve hours, despite the challenges of hard labor.) Meanwhile, Simon was busying himself, getting everything ready for the departure to hospital and making sure the house was in good order to leave for a couple of days. Miriam felt that standing up and leaning over the kitchen counter was an excellent position for her and rightly so; within minutes of taking up this position, contractions became more intense and closer together. Gravity was helping to bring that baby down onto the cervix and speed up the dilation process.

By 2:00 pm the contractions were only two to three minutes apart and lasting from one to two minutes. Each contraction was still being meticulously timed and noted by Simon who never missed a beat. It was time to call the midwives and let them know that we were coming in. Miriam found it very soothing as I talked to her during each contraction and helped her visualize what was going on in her body. For this reason, she decided to ride to the hospital in the back of my car. It was more spacious and I would be able to gently talk her through the contractions on our way to hospital. So we followed behind Simon and I kept my fingers crossed that the lights would stay green. The roads were unknown to me and I did *not* want to lose my pilot car in front.

We arrived at Hamlet Medical Center at 2:45 pm and were admitted to Room 410, which offered a pleasant view over the front of the hospital. Our first nurse was Betsy who had the unenviable task of filling out all the paper work for a new arrival. First, however, she set about hooking Miriam up to the monitors – a task she accomplished by 3:05 pm. Then, out of necessity, she started asking the dozens of apparently irrelevant questions. I appreciated the fact that Betsy was sensitive to Miriam's needs and that she waited patiently during contractions before launching into her next tirade of questions. Another nurse came in to take blood, much to Miriam's dismay, as she has very difficult veins from which to draw blood. This nurse, however, was very skilled at the task and distracted us all brilliantly by reciting the words to "Twisting the Night Away." We were all enthralled by her recitation and before we knew it, the blood had been taken.

At 4:00 pm the shift changed and Cindy, our new nurse, came in. It was a little awkward at the beginning, as she omitted introducing herself and we weren't quite sure what her role was. She turned out to be a kind and supportive teammate, however, and remained with us throughout. As soon as Miriam was able to get off the monitors she wanted to stand up again. We raised the bed to its full height, placed some three or four pillows on it. Miriam spent the large part of her labor leaning on the pillows, feet planted firmly on the floor. It was an excellent choice for her labor; she was upright, mobile, felt less pressure on her back and was able to move her pelvis rhythmically from side to side to "rock" her baby down.

Simon faithfully held the fan for her, as she was seriously overheating. Try as we might, we couldn't get the room cool enough for her. He kept hold of that fan right up until the baby appeared, never faltering in his desire to keep Miriam as comfortable as possible during those tough hours. For variety's sake, we took a tour of the corridors a couple of times and enjoyed watching the newborns in the nursery. Contractions were still coming every two minutes or so and were very intense. Miriam, however, never faltered in her ability to work with the contractions and allow her body to do its job smoothly and efficiently.

Finally, at 5:00 pm, Debby Atwater, the midwife, came in to check Miriam. She had been at 2 cm dilation twenty-four hours ago, but given that contractions had only really picked up and become stronger at about 1:00 pm, I felt it would be logical to assume that she might be 4 or 5 cm dilated by now. To our delight and amazement, Debby announced that Miriam was 8 cm dilated. Only two more centimeters to go before she would be able to push her baby out! I was so impressed that Miriam was still able to joke and chat between contractions at this late stage of labor. Many women at this stage are truly "losing it." She even read the joke to me from the side of the popsicle stick – definitely a first in my book! Miriam continued to work really hard during each contraction and I continued to talk her through them. We worked together as partners – with the sound of my voice helping her to focus on what was happening in her body.

An hour later, Debby checked her again after Miriam had told us that she was beginning to feel a lot of rectal pressure. This was an excellent sign that the baby was coming down the birth canal and perhaps she would be fully dilated and ready to push. However, on examination, she was at 9 cm and still needed one more centimeter of dilation before there would be room for the baby to come down. Debby suggested breaking the waters in order to allow the baby's head to put more pressure on the cervix, and hopefully, push that last bit of it out of the way. The fluid from the waters was clear – a sign that everything was going well for the baby. Poor Miriam was extremely uncomfortable lying on her back in the bed, which was the position she had previously assumed for the examinations. Restless, fatigued and in a good deal of pain, she moved onto her side for a while which took the pressure off her back. Despite her growing exhaustion, however, she soon decided that she absolutely *had* to be standing up again. From then on, Debby performed examinations while kneeling on the floor. How lucky we were to have such an accommodating and flexible midwife!

At 7:00 pm Debby checked her again and alas, there was still a small lip of cervix in the way preventing the baby's head from coming down any further. I could see that Debby was beginning to get a little concerned about this lip, owing to Miriam's growing exhaustion and the fact that the contractions seemed to be weakening somewhat. As a possible solution, she suggested that Miriam try pushing hard during a contraction, while Debby would attempt to manually move the lip out of the way. This is a very painful and unpleasant procedure, but Miriam bravely agreed with no hesitation. Unfortunately, this attempt was not successful and at 8:00 pm the lip was still there.

Our next strategy was to try pushing in a number of different positions. Miriam was exhausted and despondent, but she never once thought of giving up. She willingly went along with all our suggestions; she sat on the toilet, she dangled in a supported squat while leaning back against Simon who sat on the bed; she even went back to side lying. At times, Debby would insert her fingers and try to push the lip out of the way. Finally, at 8:20 pm, Debby gave me an ear-to-ear grin and nodded – the lip had disappeared and the baby's head was able to pass into the birth canal.

The hard work was not over for Miriam, however, who still had to push her baby out into the world. I have rarely seen such inner strength and tenacity in a woman. Miriam was determined to birth her baby despite her weakening contractions and growing exhaustion. She pushed with all her might for every contraction and learned how to do it more effectively by carefully listening to our suggestions. Little by little, the baby moved down and by 8:50 pm we could see a little bit of hair appearing with the contractions. Simon continued to hold the fan and marvel at the miracle occurring in front of his very eyes. Just after 9:00 pm, Anthony's head was out and we could see his beautiful face. With another major contraction and tremendous effort from Miriam, the rest of his body slipped out at 9:03 pm, guided by Debby's expert hands.

He was perfect in every way. Alert, eyes wide open and looking around at this strange new world he had come into. He lay quietly on his mother's chest as Simon cut the cord. Cindy then took him to the warmer to be weighed and measured. Meanwhile Debby cleaned Miriam up, gently delivered the placenta and gave her a couple of stitches to repair the small tear she had sustained during pushing. Anthony weighed a healthy 7lbs., 10 oz and was 19 inches long, with a head measurement of 35 cm. He was a gorgeous baby, alert and medication free. He took to the breast as soon as Cindy brought him over and suckled like a pro while I had the honor of inviting Miriam's parents in to meet their new grandson.

Words cannot describe my admiration for Miriam's ability to work with her contractions and labor with calm and confidence. She trusted the birthing process and allowed her body to be taken over with all the overwhelming feelings of labor. She never faltered in her belief of her body's innate wisdom to bring her baby safely and naturally into this world.

"Rachel's ability to concentrate was remarkable and she seemed to want silence in order to focus on the intense sensations that were occurring during each surge."

SARAH'S BIRTH

"Mind over matter." It's a common phrase we toss around without really under-standing what it means — or what it can mean. Throughout my years as a doula, I have witnessed first-hand, the human mind's astounding capability to work with labor pain. For many women, regular practice of a particular birthing technique during pregnancy enables them to cope with the intense sensations of labor. Hyp-nobirthing is the technique that Rachel utilized and I'm sure you'll be amazed — as I still am — by her calm and composed birth of Sarah.

Rachel and John were enjoying dinner out with John's parents on Sunday evening when she began to have some regular contractions at 8:00 pm. The visit to the midwife the previous Thursday had shown her to be 3 cm dilated and 85% effaced. (The cervix needs to dilate to 10 cm and reach 100% effacement in order to allow passage for the baby.) So, Rachel was well on her way to bringing her baby into the world many days before she actually went into labor. The *surges* — a kinder term used for the word "contraction" among those couples who have taken hypnobirth-ing classes — did not continue to be regular and occurred sporadically during the night. Rachel was able to sleep between the surges and so she awoke refreshed on Monday morning and sent John off to work. She assumed that the surges needed to be regular and closer together before she could really consider herself in labor.

Rachel's father in law, Al, drove her to her ultrasound at 11:00 am which showed her that everything was fine with the amniotic fluid and placenta. Next was the visit with Olivia, the midwife, who examined her and exclaimed in amazement that Rachel was now nearly 6 cm dilated and 100% effaced! She was already over half way along the labor path before even being in active labor! This is most unusual for a first time mom, who is more commonly entirely focused on her surges right from the very beginning. Rachel was clearly an exceptional woman whose ability to work with her body and relax was enabling dilation to occur with a minimum of discomfort.

Given Rachel's unexpected progress, Olivia sent her over to the hospital immedi-ately. There was no question of returning home to pick up all her belongings, which had been carefully prepared for her stay in hospital. Fortunately, she'd left an ex-tensive list on the kitchen counter, so John was able to pack for her and only forgot a couple of items in his haste! She called John who left work in a whirl and had a tough time not speeding on Interstate 78. She called me as well, and I was able to promptly cancel my one massage client of the day and I immediately headed off to Ivybridge Medical Center.

Rachel and Al settled in to Room 415 at 12:30 pm and I arrived fifteen minutes later. Rachel seemed very calm and barely noticed the surges which I noticed on the monitoring machine. The first half an hour was taken up with our nurse, Karen, who asked all the usual (and often irrelevant) inquiries about her health and previous illnesses. Rachel answered with poise and grace, despite the endless barrage of questions. Al kept us cheerful with his banter and the atmosphere was light with excitement in the air. At about 1:30 pm, John arrived and was relieved to find Rachel so calm and coping so well with her labor. Al left us once his son got settled in. Surges were now coming fairly regularly, about every five minutes, with Rachel coping beautifully.

At 2:00 pm Kathy Simms, the midwife on call, came in to introduce herself and check Rachel. She would be working with us for the afternoon until Olivia came on call at 5:30 pm. Kathy announced that Rachel was 5 to 6 cm dilated and 90% effaced with the baby's head down nice and low at 0 station. (The baby's head has to descend from -4 to +4 for delivery through the pelvis.) These figures were a little different from Olivia's examination that morning and showed us just how subjective internal exams can be. So with that assessment, it seemed that Rachel had not made any significant change since 11:30 am. The news was certainly a bit disappointing, but she did not become upset or despondent in the least.

Kathy also explained that the baby was ROA – right occiput anterior – meaning that the baby's spine was lying to the front and on the right hand side of Rachel's belly. Kathy would have preferred to see the baby LOA with the spine on the left side of Rachel's belly which would make it less likely to fall into an OP – occiput posterior – position. OP positions for the baby are best avoided because the baby's back pressing against Mom's back can slow labor down and cause severe back pain. So Kathy recommended that Rachel either remain upright and lean forward with each surge, or lie on her left side. Both of these positions would encourage the baby to move over to the left side of Rachel's belly and discourage an OP position. Surges were now becoming more intense and Rachel began to go into her deep state of relaxation that she had learned during the hypnobirthing and yoga classes.

We began to walk the corridors with Rachel stopping and focusing for each surge as they grew more intense with the walking. There wasn't much mileage to cover in the maternity area, but at least we were able to gaze at the newborns in the nursery. While strolling the hallway, Rachel and John chatted with another couple whom they had met at a "Hi, New Baby" class and who were being induced that afternoon. At 3:30 pm we returned to Room 415 and tried some different positions. Rachel positioned herself on all four's on the bed but did not seem to find that comfortable. Eventually, she ended up sitting cross-legged on the bed, leaning back against me as she breathed gently through each surge.

At 4:00 pm our new nurse Tina came on duty and took a generous amount of blood from Rachel for the cord blood donation box. We walked the corridors some more and had time to admire a set of triplet girls who had been born a few weeks earlier. At 4:20 pm, Rachel was reconnected to the monitor for a while to see how the baby was reacting to the surges. Shortly after, Kathy came by to take her leave and wish Rachel good luck with the birth. Once again, we ventured out into the corridors and paced in a clockwise direction around the square. Rachel continued to handle it all quite well, stopping with every surge and leaning forward as she held onto John for support.

Rachel's ability to concentrate was remarkable and she seemed to want silence in order to focus on the intense sensations that were occurring during each surge. At 5:30 pm, it was time to return to the monitor belts which were fitted while Rachel sat in the rocking chair. She liked this position, as the surges were gentler and more spaced out than when she was mobile. She listened to Brian Eno music and rocked rhythmically back and forth during the surges. It was ideal for taking a break, but I gently reminded her that in fact we were looking for surges *closer together* and *more intense* in order to help the labor to progress. Cheerfully, Rachel agreed to get up and move again after her brief respite in the rocking chair.

At 6:15 pm Olivia the midwife arrived and checked Rachel. She was now 8 cm dilated, perhaps only an hour or two away from pushing her baby out. The surges were becoming very intense but Rachel was still coping with each one calmly and confidently. Tina called her "a gem" and said working with Rachel was like having a breath of fresh air. Few women labor in this way, with such calm and no fear or panic, trusting implicitly in the birth process as it unfolds in all its mystery.

Rachel decided that it was time to try the whirlpool tub, in spite of the fact that it was nestled away in the farthest corner of the maternity ward. Tina filled the tub and Rachel and John set off to find it. I returned from a short dinner break and came across the pair making very slow progress towards the whirlpool. Walking was now causing the surges to come every couple of minutes. Despite the intensity, Rachel never once lost control or appeared overwhelmed by the sensations. A few slow, steady steps and then it was time to hang on to John again for another surge. And so it went, until she finally reached the blissfully warm waters of the whirlpool tub. The soothing water gave Rachel great relief from the intensity of the surges. So much so, in fact, that she might have been content to stay there for quite some time. Her labor, however, was progressing right along and some of the surges were now accompanied by a pushing sensation. So, within half an hour, Rachel opted for getting back to her room — nobody was planning on a water birth! John and I helped her out of the tub, dried her off and we shuffled back to Room 415, stopping every few yards to work with another surge.

Back in the room, Olivia examined her at 7:30 pm and announced that she was now 9 cm dilated and there was a small lip of cervix on the right hand side that was preventing full dilation. Olivia suggested either breaking the membranes, which would put more pressure on the cervix from the baby's head, or lying on her right side to force the lip out of the way. Despite the discomfort of side-lying, Rachel opted for that alternative, as her preference was to avoid the intervention of artificial rupture of the membranes for as long as possible.

By 7:50 pm, John was reading a relaxation script to her while she lay on her right side, moaning softly with each surge. The sensations were becoming so intense now, that John had to stop his reading during each surge. He was only able to continue in intervals, as each round of pain passed. Rachel had a strong urge to go to the bathroom, which is generally a positive sign that the baby is moving down deep into the pelvis. Considering this new development, Olivia checked her again and found that there was still a small lip left. With that discovery, Olivia strongly recommended breaking the membranes in order to put pressure on the lip and move it out of the way. She proceeded to rupture the waters during the examination and saw that there was light meconium in the fluid. The presence of meconium may be a sign of fetal distress, so it was clear that this baby really needed to come out into the world fairly soon.

Olivia insisted that Rachel remain on her right side. Even though, for her, this was the most uncomfortable position, Rachel stalwartly agreed to stay there for a little longer. Olivia said she could start pushing with the surges, but as of yet, Rachel did not seem to have a very strong urge to push. To help move things along, Olivia attempted to manually move the lip out of the way. The procedure had to have been extremely painful, but Rachel never complained and continued to work in harmony with her body. It was an absolutely incredible display of *mind over matter*.

Finally at 8:50 pm, Olivia announced that Rachel was completely dilated and the pushing could really begin in earnest. Rachel began in the semi reclining position and it took her a while to learn how to push effectively. She listened carefully to Olivia's helpful hints, and with our encouragement, she gradually began to push with more focus and effectiveness. John really kept Rachel on track during this very difficult phase, softly reminding her of her breathing patterns during the surges. She listened intently and responded beautifully to his caring, gentle voice. Her back was terribly painful, so she wanted to try pushing in the squatting position. Tina brought the squatting bar in and set it up on the end of the bed. This position was less painful for Rachel, but the baby's progression through the birth canal seemed to slow down. After about twenty minutes, Olivia requested that she return to the semi reclining position.

It was now 9:30 pm, a point at which Rachel's demeanor remarkably changed. All hesitation and exhaustion were suddenly subdued and she was overcome by a fierce determination to birth her baby. This manifested itself as focused, effective pushing with each powerful surge. It was then that the baby began to move. Within an hour, we could see the top of the baby's head with each surge. John's face was a picture of awe and wonderment as he caught the first glimpses of his baby's hair. Rachel continued to push bravely through the pain of the surges and shortly before 11:00 pm, the head was crowning on the perineum.

The pediatric doctor was called in (because of the light meconium) and Olivia gowned up for the birth. At the moment of crowning, the fetal heart rate sped up dramatically – an indication that the baby was no longer comfortable in that position – so Olivia was obliged to cut a small episiotomy in order to deliver the baby more quickly. At last, the entire head appeared and Olivia suctioned mucous and meconium out of the baby's mouth before moving on to delivering the shoulders.

There were a few moments of intense activity when the shoulders didn't seem to want to come out. Tina had to exert pressure on Rachel's belly while Olivia pulled fairly frantically to deliver the baby. Finally, at 11:06 pm, Sarah slipped out – a perfect baby girl with Apgars of 9 and 9 (the highest a newborn generally scores). She was immediately taken over to the crib to be checked out by the doctor while Rachel lay there, amazed that this perfect little person had just come out of her own body! Weighed and measured, she came into this world at 7 lbs. 3.6oz and 19½ inches long.

John stood next to Rachel, gazing at his daughter, falling in love as the seconds ticked by. Within a few minutes Sarah was able to snuggle onto her Mom's chest while Olivia set about delivering the placenta and stitching up the episiotomy. Sarah was alert and ready to suckle, and enjoyed her first feeding within minutes of being born. John took some photos and went out to announce the wonderful news to the family, who had been waiting anxiously outside for several hours.

It was such an honor to work with Rachel and John during this incredible journey. Rachel, you have an amazing capacity to work so cheerfully with the sensations of labor, which is rare in a first time mom. You never became despondent or lost control, and when things became especially challenging, John was always there to soothe you and get you back on track. What an amazing couple you are!

BEN'S BIRTH

Few would argue that the advances in modern medicine have approached nearly miraculous proportions. Burgeoning technologies, new techniques and an ever-expanding universe of pharmaceuticals have saved and/or prolonged countless lives worldwide. Granting all of that, there is a great deal to be said for the more natural approaches to health, healing and of course, childbirth. Many women (couples, for that matter), have a heartfelt preference for birthing their babies without modern medical intervention – or at least, with as little of it as possible. For these couples, a natural birth can be one of life's most treasured gifts for parents and newborns alike. Sarah and Joe were among the fortunate ones and were able to bring Ben into this world as nature intended.

Sarah had been having signs of labor for days: sporadic contractions; a little bloody show; some nausea and chills. Her due date had come and gone and an induction date at forty-two weeks (April 28) was looming ominously on the horizon. Things were getting serious. Sarah, who was proactive in all walks of life, wasted no time. She scheduled three acupuncture sessions to help stimulate labor. She walked incessantly in the gorgeous spring sunshine on a daily basis. Generally speaking, she attempted to move things along in every which-way possible.

By Thursday, April 23rd, she felt as if real changes were beginning to occur with mild but regular contractions and more of the "bloody show." She walked, she rested, she took a bath, and she ate nutritious food *for her baby and her.* (That sentence will forever be in my mind from the hypnobirthing CD!) She then went to bed, hoping that stronger contractions would awake her in the middle of the night. Alas, this was not to be. In fact, she slept very well, which turned out to be a blessing, given that sleep was totally elusive the following night.

Friday followed a similar pattern to Thursday, with contractions coming mild and regular throughout the day, more bloody show, more walking, more resting, and more nutritious food for mom and baby. By about 5:00 pm the contractions were definitely beginning to pick up in intensity and regularity. Joe and Sarah felt they were *finally* on their way to having a baby. We spoke on the phone at 9:00 pm and were all fully expecting to be getting together at some point during the night, as contractions continued to increase.

The next call from Sarah was at 11:50 pm announcing that contractions had been three to five minutes apart for quite a while and it was time for me to come over and join them. At 12:10 am, I was half way to their house in Highton Park when my phone rang again. It was Sarah, who said that they had decided to go straight to the hospital, given the regularity and timing of the contractions – and could I meet them there? A moment of panic, as I, without a GPS (and with only Google map directions to their house), tried to figure out how to get from Amley Road to Plymouth, a route I had never taken. Fortunately, I took a random right turn and hit Route 28 almost immediately, which put me back in familiar territory. It would have been a fine thing for the doula to get lost and miss all the action!

I arrived at Plymouth Medical Center at a half past midnight, but there was no sign of Joe and Sarah. A quick phone call revealed that they had left some bags at home and had returned to pick them up. They would be arriving at the hospital shortly after 1:00 am. Joe parked the car in front of the emergency entrance and we unloaded all their bags. Sarah was looking cheerful and excited and coping well with the contractions. We ferried all the bags up to Room 443 where Sharon, our friendly nurse, helped us get settled in. A barrage of questions ensued. Many of them seemed completely irrelevant to having a baby, but Sarah answered each one with patience, despite the fact that she was preoccupied with the contractions. She put on the ubiquitous hospital gown – a gown so complicated in design, with its snaps and nursing slits, that we had it all askew until the experienced Sharon came in and got Sarah's arms through the correct openings.

Karen was to be our midwife for the weekend and she arrived at about 2:30 am to check Sarah and assess what was going on. She announced that Sarah was 2 cm dilated and 80% effaced. (In order to birth the baby, the cervix needs to efface from 0 to 100%, and dilate from 0 to 10 cm and the baby has to move down from -4 through 0 to +4 station.) Three days prior to this, she had been 1 to 2 cm dilated and 50% effaced. This news must have been disappointing for Joe and Sarah. After two days of contractions they might have hoped to be closer to 4 cm. However, the body works in mysterious ways and it is very normal for first time moms to require several days of preparation work before labor really kicks in.

Karen said that she would not admit Sarah, given that it was so early in the process, but that she would not send her home immediately either, since it was the middle of the night. She suggested waiting two hours and checking again. If there was any change at all, she would allow her to stay. On the other hand, if her cervix was still at 2 cm and 80% effaced, she would send us home to wait for active labor to begin. This news was clearly disappointing for Sarah and Joe, who had hoped they were well on their way. To their credit, however, they did not become despondent and immediately suggested lots of walking in order to keep the contractions coming stronger.

With that, Sarah and I walked around the maternity ward in endless circles – past the nursery where we could peep in between the shutters and see three newborns, past the nurses' station where their lively chit chat belied the early hour. When she felt tired, Sarah would return to her room and sit on the birth ball, swaying gently from side to side to encourage the baby to rotate and move down through the pelvis. Joe wisely took this opportunity to snooze before the action started. At 5:00 am, Karen checked Sarah again and we waited with baited breath. She was now 3 cm dilated and although Karen generally preferred to admit her patients at 4 cm, she recommended that we stay. She felt it would be better for us to get some rest before active labor began, plus, we wouldn't have to drive back and forth at such an ungodly hour.

Sarah settled in to bed, Joe on the pullout chair and I made myself comfortable with sheets and blankets. We put on the hypnobirthing CD that Sarah and Joe had been practicing with for weeks. The soporific, soothing voice of the British woman reading the text was mesmerizing and we were all immediately quiet and relaxed. For the next two hours we dozed and relaxed. Sarah breathed gently through her surges as she became increasingly confident, empowered and relaxed by the spellbinding CD.

At around 7:00 am our new nurse Aileen introduced herself and checked Sarah's vitals. Her blood pressure was a little high, but registered a lower reading on the second check. Absolutely everyone who attended to Sarah commented on her underwear, which had "Baby" printed all over it. It was a sad moment when Sarah felt it was time to change into ordinary red underwear and lose the admiring comments of nurses and midwives! The contractions became stronger and were getting closer together, especially when Sarah stood or moved around. So at 7:45 am, she and Joe went off to walk the corridors for a while.

At 8:15 am Karen returned to perform another examination. To our joy and delight, she announced that Sarah was now 5 cm dilated and 90% effaced! This was wonderful news and we now felt we were well and truly on our way. Contractions were definitely becoming more intense and Sarah coped beautifully — moaning quietly, almost a hum, as she breathed slowly and deeply and swayed her hips to the power of the surges. We were momentarily offered a slight change of atmosphere when two technicians came in to draw Sarah's blood. They were very cheerful and chatted away to each other in Hindi as they expertly drew her blood for lab work and then wished us good luck in English.

At 8:40 am Sarah took a shower to freshen up. To her delight (as delighted as one can be in this situation), the warm water eased the intensity of the contractions. By now Sarah was truly in active labor and resting in the bed was an absolute impossibility. At this point, she decided to try using the TENS unit, which would serve as a mild distraction to the other sensations in her body. TENS stands for Transcutaneous Electrical Nerve Stimulation. With the unit's stimulating pads placed strategically on the laboring woman's back, it offers mild electrical impulses. These impulses "tingle" to varying degrees (depending on the desired setting) and divert attention away from the sensations of labor. It is a device that is commonly used in maternity wards in Canada, Australia and the UK.

Sarah spent a lot of time rocking on the birth ball with Joe sitting in a chair behind her, gently stroking her back and encouraging her with words of love and admiration. Despite the intensity of the contractions she remained incredibly "loosey-goosey" and unperturbed — sighing and moaning gently and visualizing her body softening and opening for her baby. She was getting some pain from muscles in her left hip which continued to dog her throughout the entire labor. The hot pack helped a little, as did the occasional pressure from my fist or a tennis ball. Nothing, unfortunately, would completely relieve the unpleasant sensation that shot down her left leg.

At 10:30 am she was required to return to bed for some more monitoring. Again, she put on the hypnobirthing CD and relaxed beautifully — no small feat for a woman in active labor. The soothing message that emanated from the CD spoke in sharp contrast to the turmoil Sarah was experiencing. On one hand, the voice was saying, "You are calm. Your baby is calm." And on the other hand, the baby was doing what sounded like somersaults inside her! Once the monitor belts had been removed, she preferred to stand up and lean against Joe, swaying from side to side in rhythm with her surges. It was the most beautiful labor dance, so close and intimate and in perfect synchrony with each other.

At 11:30 am, Karen checked her once more and she was now 6 cm dilated. Slow, steady progress was being made, which was perfectly normal for a first labor. Everything was right on track. By this time, however, the contractions had become so intense that Sarah decided it was time to get into the bath – also known as "the midwives' epidural." First of all, we had to take the stimulating pads from the TENS unit off of her back, as this is not compatible with being in the water. We went across the corridor into the bathroom at 11:45 am and it was lovely: candles (albeit ones run by battery); lavender aromatherapy oil; low lights and music. This all helped Sarah relax in the warm water as the jets gently massaged her back.

Joe took this opportunity to go and get some lunch (especially the pudding he was craving) and Karen and I sat quietly with Sarah as she continued to labor beautifully in the bathtub. Then it was my turn to get some lunch and I returned to them at 12:50 pm, after a scary five minutes of locking myself in the men's bathroom (that's another story). I found the earlier, serene atmosphere had changed into a scene of emotional upheaval. Overwhelmed and distraught, Sarah was questioning her ability to give birth. It took all the love and encouragement from Joe and reassurance from Karen to calm her down. (This is absolutely normal for a woman in labor to experience an emotional rollercoaster from one moment to the next.) When I stepped into the bathroom Karen whispered to me, with a big grin on her face, "She's moving into transition and having a meltdown!" Midwives view this kind of behavior as an excellent sign that things are moving along fast and are not in the least bit disturbed by tears of anger and frustration.

Once back in her room, Karen checked her again and immediately realized why Sarah was feeling so confused and upset. The baby had moved down two whole centimeters during Sarah's bath hour! This meant that there was an enormous amount of pressure and pain, as the baby's head stretched and pushed all the ligaments and muscles of the pelvis out of the way. Sarah, however, was still at 6 cm of dilation. This was distressing for her to hear. The progress had been in the baby's descent and there was no change in the cervix. Actually, this is not uncommon during labor, which rarely occurs in a textbook-style linear progression. Laboring moms, however, tend to focus on the dilation number and get discouraged if it is not changing.

Contractions were coming fierce and strong now and Sarah needed to try several different positions in order to work with the overwhelming sensations that were roaring through her body. She went on all fours on the bed for a while and also sat on the birth ball a lot, but most of the time she stood and danced her labor dance with Joe, who held her tightly. Between contractions she would slowly lower herself into the rocking chair and Joe would rest in the chair next to her. As soon as another contraction came, he would lift her up and she would put her arms around his neck. Together they would sway – he a pillar of strength, she rocking and moaning, and undulating her pelvis to bring her baby down further and further.

Karen and I wished we could have taped this exquisite ritual to use it as a birth DVD for expectant parents. They worked in perfect harmony while Karen and I did no more than hold the sacred space for them to work together in peace and quiet. Karen, as yet unmarried and with no kids, whispered to me "I hope I find a partner who works with me with such devotion during labor." I hope she does too – they are a rare gift.

By now Sarah's waters had broken – not a gush of forewater (in front of the baby's head) but a trickle of hindwater (behind the baby's head). There was light meconium in the water. This meant that a neonatologist would have to be present at the birth, in order to suction the baby immediately to avoid aspirating any meconium. This news must have been disappointing for Sarah and Joe as they had their hearts set on immediate bonding with their baby on Sarah's chest. They, of course, understood the importance of taking all precautions to avoid breathing problems and accepted the news. The meconium also meant that Karen was going to have to monitor Sarah continuously until the birth – yet another precaution, as the presence of meconium can sometimes indicate that the baby is in distress. Karen was not the least bit surprised that there was light meconium, as the baby was ten days overdue and this is common for a late baby. So there was no cause for alarm, but it must have been difficult for Sarah to have to contend with two monitor belts being continuously strapped round her belly. Compared to the intensity of the contractions and the shooting pain in her left leg, however, it was an insignificant annoyance.

Sarah and Joe continued working hard with the labor – Sarah's moan sometimes rising in pitch to contend with the increasing intensity of contractions. She would occasionally rock her pelvis furiously as if trying to shake the baby down. These were among the most intense moments of her labor. At one point, she actually lifted her legs off the ground, swinging in mid air as she clung to Joe. Always her "rock," Joe continued to be grounded and calm, despite the emotional turmoil Sarah was experiencing. He would often quietly peruse his book *The Birth Partner* by Penny Simkin, checking for information and seeing if there were any other ideas he could come up with to help Sarah. Joe was very knowledgeable and as Karen pointed out, had clearly done all his homework.

At 3:15 pm, Karen came in to check Sarah again and break the bag of forewaters. The baby was really low in the pelvis but Sarah was still at 6 cm. Before Sarah could become disheartened, Karen quickly explained that now the forewaters had disappeared, the baby's head would be able to press down directly onto the cervix. This was sure to cause quick dilation. Indeed, the pressure became ever more intense and Sarah had to muster up all her courage and energy to keep working with her fierce contractions.

At 3:40 pm, Sarah began to feel the urge to push, so Karen hastily checked her again. She was now 8 cm and opening up to 9 cm with each contraction. What wonderful news that she had changed from 6 cm to 9 cm in only twenty minutes! No wonder Sarah was feeling overwhelmed. She was going through transition, the toughest part of labor, at lightning speed. Indeed, one of her first comments when we began chatting about the birth afterwards was "transition really sucks." Many women would second that!

Karen suggested that Sarah lie on her right side, as there was some cervix remaining on the right. If she lay on that side, the greater pressure from the baby's head might get rid of the lip. At 4 pm, the small lip was still there but only between contractions. At Karen's request Sarah struggled not to push, because pushing fiercely could potentially put so much pressure on the remaining cervix that it would swell up. In such instances, the cervix can actually close down instead of opening up. Being told not to push when you have an overwhelming urge to do so is like being told there are no bathrooms available when you have a bad case of the stomach flu! Sarah struggled to pant and breathe through her contractions in order to avoid pushing and did a fantastic job.

Finally, at 4:15 pm, Karen gave her permission to push with all her might, as the lip had moved out of the way and she was truly fully dilated. This must have been a huge relief to Sarah, whose body was so expert in following the needs of her labor. First she pushed in the side-lying position and then, after fifteen minutes, tried using the squatting bar in order to utilize gravity. The baby, however, did not tolerate the squatting position and the heart rate dropped dramatically. So, Karen quickly got her to move into a semi-reclining position and use the oxygen mask for a few contractions to get the baby back on track. Sarah pushed very effectively. Within twenty-five minutes, we could already spot the top of the baby's head with each contraction. She bravely pushed through the intense "ring of fire" as the baby's head stretched the skin with each push.

The neonatologist quietly came in and introduced himself. Karen continued to coach Sarah through each contraction while Joe stayed at her head and whispered constant words of encouragement in her ear. At 4:47 pm, Ben Richard Ramsey slipped out with the cord compressed against his shoulder. This explained the heart rate dropping in the squatting position, as he must have been compressing the cord against the wall of the birth canal. Karen immediately cut the cord and I raised his leg to show Sarah the sex. He was then whisked off to the crib to be suctioned and checked out. The neonatologist quickly announced him to be in perfect shape and the nurse weighed and measured him. He weighed 7 lbs 6oz and was 20¾ inches long with Apgars of 9 and 9 at birth – the highest a newborn ever scores.

Once the preliminaries had been completed Joe was able to hold Ben while Karen delivered the placenta and checked the bleeding. She gave Sarah just one stitch to repair a small tear. And then at 5:15 pm, the big moment came when Sarah was able to hold her son to her chest and nurse him and talk to him. He fed lustily and had no problem latching on. Little Ben was very alert, taking in his new surroundings and responding to the loving voices of his mom and dad.

Sarah and Joe, what an adventure that day was for the two of you – all your hard work worth every moment, once you were able to hold and cherish your beautiful baby. Your determination to avoid medications and unnecessary interventions never faltered, even through the most challenging times. Your support of one another was remarkable and Ben is a lucky boy to have such devoted and loving parents. Thank you for allowing me the honor of being witness to this incredible day and helping you to experience the perfectly natural birth of Ben.

VERONICA'S BIRTH

Life is filled with decisions. Day in and day out, most of them seem obvious or small. Occasionally, they appear to be more significant, and every once in a while, they feel truly cumbersome. All of us, I'm sure, strive to make the wisest decisions possible, based on the best information that's available. That would probably to be true, at least, when it comes to "the big ones." What we tend to forget, however, is that any decision, big or small, can be a life changer. As with everything else, childbirth is fraught with decisions of every size. Expectant parents, Jessica and Andres, were faced with a situation during Jessica's labor. Considering the best available information, they made what appeared to be a very obvious decision. It turned out to be one that they – and I – will never forget.

Jessica began having mild contractions at about midnight on Tuesday morning January 20. Although regular, they remained consistently short in length and did not seem to become stronger, closer together and longer lasting as time went on. At about 4:00 am, however, they started occurring every two minutes and Jessica and Andres were beginning to feel that they were occurring frequently enough to warrant a journey to the hospital. Andres called me at 4:20 am to let me know that things were moving along. They were waiting for Jessica's mom to arrive to take care of three-year-old Olivia before leaving for the hospital. The couple set out for Brixham Medical Center at 5:30 am and I met them there at 6:00 am.

Our first nurse was a cheery soul by the name of Meg who examined Jessica at 6:30 am and pronounced her to be about 2 cm dilated, 50% effaced and the baby still fairly high at -2 station. The cervix has to efface to 100%, to dilate to 10 cm and the baby moves from -4 through 0 to +4 station. This news must have been disappointing for Jessica and Andres because her previous examination four days prior had proffered much the same result. In other words, there had been little change despite several hours of regular contractions. Neither Jessica nor Andres, however, revealed the least hint of despondency. They continued to be in good spirits and as optimistic as always. Endless forms were half-read and signed. Contractions were coming every four minutes and Jessica got herself nicely settled on the birthing ball for a while, hips swaying to the rhythm of the contractions.

At eight o'clock we were allocated our new nurse, Beth, who was very likeable, but had an insensitive habit of chatting during contractions. Andres and Jessica focused on the contractions and I occasionally offered Beth a polite smile, but none of us were really listening to her! Dr. Blacksell arrived at 8:20 am and examined Jessica again. This time she was two-to-three centimeters dilated, still 50% effaced and the baby was pronounced to be a little lower at 0 station. Dr Blacksell suggested that this baby had been at 0 station four days ago and it was simply Jessica's position on the bed that had caused Meg to estimate the baby at -2 station. Her assessment implied that in two hours, no major changes had taken place despite regular contractions. Jessica and Andres seemed not in the least perturbed by this news and were willing to allow nature to take its course, however slowly.

For the next hour, Jessica wallowed in the warm whirlpool tub, the jets massaging her back and Andres splashing water over her belly during contractions. They were calm and peaceful and perfectly content with their labor of love. At ten o'clock I went down to the cafeteria to get Andres some breakfast and when I returned they were both resting peacefully in their room, knowing that they had many hours of wakefulness ahead of them. I moved their minivan before it got towed away from the emergency entrance, never suspecting the momentous events that would occur there a mere eighteen hours later.

At 10:45 am, after a good rest, we took to walking the corridors again. The three of us stopped for each contraction, as Jessica leaned against Andres, who whispered words of encouragement. My role in those moments was to put pressure on her lower back. Thus unfolded the course for the next few hours. Sometimes the contractions were a little stronger, sometimes they were a little farther apart. But all in all, the sensations remained fairly mild. We fell into a cycle of walking, resting, lying in the whirlpool, sitting on the birth ball, in the rocking chair. By moving around in this way, Jessica was doing everything possible to get the contractions to last longer and become more effective. Andres never left her side and was always ready with loving words of encouragement and praise.

At 1:15 pm, Dr. Blacksell examined Jessica again and she was still at 3 cm and 50% effaced. No real progress had taken place since her last check five hours ago. This was not good news, but Jessica and Andres remained as patient as ever, trusting that her body would birth her baby when it was ready. Jessica sat in the rocking chair while I gave her a foot massage and Andres went to get some lunch. At 2:15 pm, it was walkabout time again. The corridors and nurses' faces were becoming familiar to the three of us on our monotonous route – our only variation being whether to choose a clockwise or counterclockwise direction.

At 3:30 pm, Dr. Blacksell examined Jessica yet again and announced that she was *still* at 3 cm and a little more effaced at 80%. Things were moving in the right direction, but very slowly. Dr. Blacksell suggested that Jessica either receive some Pitocin to bring the labor on, or go home to rest and wait until things picked up on their own. The decision seemed obvious. Without any hesitation, Jessica and Andres opted for patience and honoring her body to do what was needed in its own time. So, we packed up our bags and left the hospital at 4:00 pm, not forgetting to stop at the gift shop and buy a soft toy monkey for Olivia. Admirably, despite this huge setback, Jessica and Andres were as cheerful as ever and totally accepting of the situation.

The couple went home and napped for a couple of hours, ate something and put Olivia to bed at her usual time. They went back to bed with the intention of getting some sleep, but at 10:00 pm, Jessica's contractions suddenly became much stronger and lasted much longer. She must have known in her heart that this was the *real thing*. She and Andres worked hard with these contractions for several hours riding the waves and overwhelming sensations with courage and a stalwart calm. Andres helped ease the pain by using strong counter-pressure on her lower back, while offering words of encouragement and support. He phoned me at 1:45 am to say that the contractions were becoming overwhelming and that the two of them could use some help. I was at their house shortly after 2:00 am and one look at Jessica told me that she was already in transition!

No time was to be lost, so Andres quickly and efficiently got everything ready in the minivan. With incredible foresight and good sense, he put the middle seat down and fitted out the rear seat with a pile of clean towels and blankets. We got Jessica onto the toilet before leaving for the hospital and I noticed that her moaning was changing during the contraction – *from a cry of pain, to a low growl of pushing!* Things were moving along so fast; we had to get to the hospital immediately. It was 2:30 am and she was in a lot of pain, but we managed to get her downstairs and dressed for the road. We half-dragged her to the van and she crawled in on all fours, ending up with her head and upper body on the rear seat, while kneeling on the floor. I wedged myself in behind her and we were off!

Her contractions were coming fast and furious by now and it was clear that she was beginning to push. I tried to encourage her to pant during a contraction and told her to keep a hold of this baby until we got to the hospital, but to no avail. While Andres drove us expertly closer to our destination, Jessica was *way beyond* listening to logic or reasoning. At 2:45 am, a powerful contraction raged through her body and she announced in no uncertain terms that her waters had broken and her baby was coming! I indecorously pulled down her pants to expose her buttocks, but none of us cared by this stage.

Sure enough, with the next contraction, I could see the bulge of a baby's head on the perineum. She really was having this baby *right now!* With the next contraction at 2:50 am, Veronica's head appeared and I held her gently, waiting for the next contraction to come. Time seemed to stand still as she looked up at me with great serenity in her eyes and a slightly quizzical expression as if to say: "Don't worry, I'm here and everything is fine." With the next contraction, her perfect little body slipped out into my hands. There were cries of jubilation from Andres, our expert dad and driver, who never faltered in his attempts to get us to the hospital quickly and safely.

Jessica was immediately composed and calm after the storm of birth and we shuffled about awkwardly on the floor of the car, trying to get her into a position where she could hold Veronica. There wasn't much room, but we managed it. Soon she was sitting on a clean towel on the floor, leaning against the rear seat and cuddling Veronica to her belly. I covered her in lots of towels and blankets to keep her warm and she contentedly nestled in to her mom's arms. Mother and baby blissfully gazed at each other while Andres drove us the last ten minutes to the hospital.

Jessica and Veronica were taken to the emergency room on a stretcher with the umbilical cord still attached. A huge throng of medics appeared from nowhere, like bees buzzing round a honey pot. They clearly weren't used to having a mother and newborn arrive in such a manner. We created quite a stir! At 3:10 am, Andres cut the cord and then went upstairs with Veronica and Jessica, and I followed shortly after.

Dr. Blacksell arrived looking a little frazzled. She too, was not used to such events and told us that Jessica was her first patient to deliver in the car. There was yet another round of paperwork with Diane, Jessica's "favorite" nurse who had been with her and Andres at Olivia's birth. How ironic that they should end up with her again.

Dr. Blacksell delivered Jessica's placenta and stitched her up. Finally, Veronica was able to come to her mother and nurse to her heart's content. She was hungry and strong and soon brought her blood sugar up with a good feeding. Slowly, things began to settle down and I left the tired but happy family at 5:00 am, hoping that they would finally be able to get some much-deserved sleep.

Jessica's dogged determination, coupled with Andres's unfailing support, got her through all the ups and downs of a challenging labor. I admire you both so much for your tenacity, good sense and strength during this labor of love. I feel honored to have been part of your exciting adventure. Thank you for allowing me to support you during this special experience. It will forever remain one of the most memorable and exhilarating events in my life. Your unfailing support for one another will enable you to meet life's challenges with courage and conviction, just as it did during the birth of Veronica. You make an awesome couple!

Births with medical INTERVENTIONS

"She allowed herself a time of deep grief as she said goodbye to her ideal birth and then embraced the new birth plan with enthusiasm and good grace."

MELANIE'S BIRInT

Time and time again, I am reminded of the fact that "life" is not bound to pay heed to our well-made plans, or to honor even the best of our intentions. As disappointing – or even frightening – as the unexpected can be, we are often left no choice but to do just one thing…roll with the changes.

Such was the case when Elspeth's waters broke in the kitchen at 3:00 pm on Friday afternoon, August 31st. That morning, she'd been at the Birth Center for an NST (non-stress test) to check that the baby was still doing fine. An hour later her water broke. She and Sam returned to the Birth Center for further NST's and to discuss what might happen next. Ruptured membranes "start the clock" so to speak, and put the mother on a time line, as there is an increased risk of infection in the uterus, especially when vaginal exams are performed. As part of the standard procedure in such cases, the midwives recommended that antibiotics be started after eighteen hours if the baby had not yet been born. Having received the necessary information and assurances, Elspeth and Sam were home again by 9:00 pm and she was already having mild contractions every so often. They were so excited by the realization that their baby was going to be born within hours – *quite a few hours* as it turned out!

All night long Elspeth continued having contractions and by early morning they were coming about three minutes apart and growing in intensity. At 6:30 am I received a phone call from Sam, letting me know what was going on. After calling the Birth Center, they were advised to come on in, so we agreed to all meet there at 7:30 am. When I arrived, Elspeth's midwife Patsy was checking her. They were in the room that had a birthing tub and the atmosphere was one of calm and relaxation. When a contraction came, Elspeth would stop talking and focus on what was going on in her body by breathing and gently moaning. Between contractions, she was still able to chat and laugh and the air was filled with a mixture of excitement and quiet confidence. Sam was constantly attentive to her needs and was always there to hold her hand and just be next to her in his quiet unassuming manner.

At 8:10 am Patsy examined Elspeth and to our great delight, discovered that she was already 5 – 6 cm dilated. This was excellent news and it meant that the first stage of her labor was progressing really well – and quite fast, as the previous evening she had not been dilated at all. By now, contractions were becoming more intense as she moved into the active labor stage. The chatting between contractions was winding down – a sure sign of active labor. Elspeth decided she might be more comfortable in the birthing tub, soothed by the warm water as it washed over her body. With each contraction, she began to gently sway in the water – her head moving rhythmically from side to side, her eyes closed, with a look of intense concentration on her face. She was going into that "other state" that women find at the time in their labors, when they need to delve into their inner resources and discover the innate power of birthing that lies deep within them. Sam would wipe Elspeth's face with a cool washcloth between contractions. Silence reigned in the room, except for the swish swashing of the water against Elspeth's belly and her gentle moans with each contraction.

At 9:00 am – 18 hours since her water broke – Patsy had to start an IV drip in order to give Elspeth her first dose of antibiotics. Much to Elspeth's dismay (and ours as well), the right arm availed nothing and the poor woman had to be poked again in the left arm in order to find a large open vein. Once the IV was started, we took turns holding the bag of antibiotics above Elspeth as she continued to labor beautifully in the tub. Thoroughly tired out from a sleepless night, she would doze between contractions and allow the warm water to relax and soothe her. It was beautiful to watch.

At 10:45 am, Rachel arrived from Linton Medical Center (LMC). She was a young midwife who had come along to watch a Birth Center birth. Rachel's energy was very positive and invigorating and I think it was helpful that she came in, just when Elspeth was beginning to feel spent. Elspeth moved into the rocking chair at 11:15 am where she spent 45 minutes rocking through each contraction and we sat watching her patiently, in awe of what was going on inside her body. At midday, she decided she would go back into the tub, as contractions were becoming quite intense and were accompanied by pressure – a sign that the baby was moving down and that Elspeth must be close to full dilation (10 cm).

Patsy examined Elspeth at 12:30 pm and announced that she was about 9 cm with an "anterior lip." This meant that the cervix was not quite dilated at the front and there was a part of it still covering the baby's head, preventing the baby from coming down any farther. Elspeth was told, however, that if she had an urge to push, she could start doing so. She began pushing at about 12:45 pm, but I could see that the urge was not overwhelming. By 1:30 pm there was little change and curiously, Elspeth's contractions were getting farther apart. With all intentions to avoid a "holding pattern" in her labor, it was suggested that she try nipple stimulation. This encourages a release of oxytocin, the hormone that brings on contractions. We all received a glimmer of renewed hope, as we observed a small response from the nipple stimulation, but contractions still needed to be closer together and more powerful. The midwives suggested that Elspeth try the birthing stool, which would put her in a more upright position, and perhaps gravity would increase the intensity of the contractions. For several excruciating contractions, Rachel attempted to move the anterior lip out of the way manually. Finally, with Rachel's help, Elspeth's cervix was fully dilated and ready to allow for the baby to pass through. By now, however, Elspeth was getting really exhausted and her uterus was fast losing its power to contract effectively.

At 3:00 pm, Elspeth moved back to the bed to lie on her side, too exhausted to sit up on the birthing stool. With each contraction, Sam would lift her upper leg and she would use what little remaining strength she possessed to bear down. Despite her heroic efforts, the baby remained high. We tried nipple stimulation again as she rested on her back, semi reclining in the bed. Rachel had to return to the hospital and it seemed like we were in limbo for an hour – Elspeth courageously pushing and the baby remaining high in the pelvis.

Shortly after 4:00 pm, Patsy began to talk about alternatives. It was clear that Elspeth urgently needed to rest, having had little sleep the previous night and having worked so hard in labor for so many long hours. Moreover, her contractions no longer seemed to be effective in bringing her baby down. She explained that there were medications available to help Elspeth rest and to increase the power and strength of her contractions. One option was that she could take a small dose of narcotic and remain at the Birth Center. In doing so, she would hopefully sleep a little and then Patsy could reassess the situation. Or, Elspeth could go over to LMC, have some kind of pain medication (either a narcotic or an epidural) and start some Pitocin, a well-known brand name of synthetic oxytocin, to increase the strength of contractions in an exhausted uterus.

It was at this point, that "life" deviated from Elspeth and Sam's well-intended plans. Neither option was in line with their birth preferences. They had their hearts set on a natural birth at the Birth Center and the idea of transferring to the hospital was, to say the least, distressing. It seemed like an impossible decision for them. They talked over the situation with Patsy and with each other, and with tears in their eyes, opted for an immediate transfer to LMC. Staying at the Birth Center to rest would have merely delayed the agonizing decision by a couple of hours and caused an already long labor to become even more drawn out. Turning their backs on their ideal natural birth they bravely chose to "roll with the changes." Embracing a new and alien world of hospitals and medication was incredibly hard for Elspeth and Sam, but they never faltered in their decision, knowing that it was their most sensible and safest choice.

At 4:40 pm, Elspeth put on her robe and we helped her walk out to her car. Sam drove the short distance to the Labor and Delivery Unit at LMC and throughout this time, Elspeth was having painful contractions but no longer had the energy to bear down. She felt so despondent and the pain must have felt much worse, in that it no longer seemed like a productive pain.

We settled into a very pleasant Room 185 – spacious and comfortable despite the obvious hospital accoutrements. The nurses, Nancy and Lynn, were kind and friendly and did their best to accommodate Elspeth's wishes. Elspeth had decided to have an epidural so that she could rest completely and allow Pitocin to be started in her IV drip, which would cause her contractions to gradually increase in frequency and intensity. Dr Sanchez came to administer the epidural, which in spite of the proce-dure's obvious benefits, required Elspeth to endure a very unpleasant ten minutes. Exhausted and in pain, she had to curl over and remain absolutely still despite her contractions so that Dr Sanchez could insert the needle into the epidural space in her back. Sam firmly held her shoulders and gave her the emotional and physical support she needed to endure the procedure. Meanwhile, Rachel returned briefly to offer her support. It must have been reassuring for Elspeth to see a familiar face again, but unfortunately, Rachel had to leave fairly quickly to attend the birth of an-other baby. Finally, at 6:00 pm, the epidural mercifully started to cause numbness in the lower part of Elspeth's body and a small amount of Pitocin was added to the IV.

Once the epidural fully kicked in, Elspeth's natural good humor and optimism swiftly returned, even though what was happening to her was so opposite to everything she had wished for. She allowed herself a time of deep grief as she said goodbye to her ideal birth and then embraced the new birth plan with enthusiasm and good grace. What a healthy and admirable attitude! It was fabulous to see her smiling and joking again. In fact, she had us all laughing as she told us about the Sheela-na-gig, a Celtic statue representing fertility whose huge vulva dominates the figure. During the next two hours, Elspeth was able to rest and even sleep a little, and Sam and I took advantage of the situation to refuel and rest. I must say that this move over to LMC was devastating for Sam too, but he never faltered in his support for Elspeth. Throughout her labor, he always seemed determined to make the best out of what must have at times appeared to be a hopeless situation.

At 7:00 pm, the nurse's shift changed and we were assigned Bobbi, who had previously been a nurse at the Birth Center. She was very sympathetic to Elspeth's needs and was clearly the right choice for them. In fact once Elspeth started pushing again at around 8:30 pm, it almost seemed like we were back at the Birth Center. Here we were, with that same experience of a loving support team patiently waiting for Elspeth's contractions to carry her along the path to delivery. Patsy tied a knot in a sheet, which she wrapped around the squatting bar at the end of the bed. With each contraction, Sam and I would hold one leg each while Elspeth grabbed on to the sheet and pulled up a little to curl around her baby. At the same time, Patsy leaned back so that Elspeth had something to pull against. This system worked well and with each contraction, Elspeth seemed to get more adept at pushing her baby out.

By 10:30, however, Elspeth was beginning to get exhausted again. Although the baby had moved down a little, progress was still very slow. Patsy said she felt it would be a good idea to allow Dr. Jennifer Rangold to come in and assess the situation, and possibly help deliver Elspeth's baby with a vacuum extraction. Once again, life was playing by a different set of rules and Elspeth was thrust into a situation that she had never imagined would happen. With a tremendous display of good grace, she agreed that this was the best option.

Dr. Rangold arrived shortly after 11:00 pm and, after an examination, stated that she felt a vacuum extraction was worth trying. We all understood that the next option was a cesarean birth — much more invasive and even more traumatic for Elspeth than a vacuum extraction. Dr. Rangold explained that she would give it two tries and then reassess if it didn't work. On the first contraction, she attempted to fit the vacuum on the baby's head and get it into the proper position. The next contraction came and with Sam and I each holding a leg, Dr. Rangold and Elspeth gave everything they had to help the baby to come out.

It took an incredible push on Elspeth's part and some very forceful pulling on the doctor's part, but finally at 11:23 pm, Melanie was born and immediately placed on Elspeth's abdomen. The joy and relief was overwhelming and it was wonderful to watch Elspeth and Sam bond with their daughter despite the flurry of medical activity still going on. Elspeth had suffered quite a bad tear and was promptly stitched while Melanie was checked out by the nursing staff. Her Apgars were 7 and 8 at birth and then rose as she quickly recovered from her difficult journey into the world. Perfect and beautiful in every way, she weighed a hefty 7 lb.-15oz and measured 19 inches long.

Finally, by 2:00 am, the ruckus had died down and the four of us were left alone to contemplate the miracle of Melanie, who by now had nursed and was settling down to a well-deserved sleep. Elspeth and Sam showed courage in the tough decisions they had had to make that day. Piece by precious piece, they had to let go of their plans for an "ideal birth." Rolling with the changes that life presented, they courageously embraced an unexpected world of hospitals and interventions. Together they inspired us all, as they showed flexibility and openness to those unpredictable events. What a life-changing day to remember!

TIMOTHY'S BIRTH

I will forever be amazed by the courage, strength and endurance of women as they labor to give birth. Every birth, of course, is a testament to female fortitude, but this is especially true of women who experience labors that are exceptionally difficult – and at times, seem to have no end in sight. Such was the case for Sally.

At 3:00 am on Monday morning, Sally woke up with some cramping and noticed a bloody show when she got up to go to the bathroom. In and of itself, this did not necessarily mean that labor was about to begin imminently, but it was a positive sign that things were moving in the right direction and the cervix was softening and effacing. (The cervix has to efface, or thin, from 0 to 100% while opening from 0 to 10 cm in order to allow the baby passage through the pelvis during labor.) She dozed in bed until 6:00 am, unable to sleep soundly because of the cramping that occurred every few minutes. The day continued in this vein with Sally feeling restless and uncomfortable, excited and nervous, anticipating the long-awaited arrival of her baby. Bill went off to work, as it was clear that this was a preliminary phase when the body is gearing up for the task ahead. It's known as a "Slow to Start Labor" and it occurs fairly frequently with first-time moms. It's a challenging part of the labor process, as mom is too uncomfortable to be easily distracted and yet active labor is still a long way ahead.

I went over in the afternoon at 3:00 pm to keep Sally company. It was a sunny, windy spring day and we went out for a lovely stroll around the neighborhood. I gave Sally a foot massage, focusing especially on the reflexology areas of her feet that stimulate the uterus and may help bring labor on. Sally said that the obvious reaction to my touch was that it made the baby move, but it didn't seem to bring contractions on any stronger. Bill returned home at 4:30 pm, so I left the two together to prepare for the incredible journey ahead. They had some dinner and Sally took a bath and tried to relax as much as possible between the contractions, which by now were coming regularly, about 5 to 7 minutes apart. It *seemed* like things were moving along.

Given that night was drawing in and we were expecting some change to happen in the early hours, we decided that I should return to Sally and Bill's house at 10:00 pm to avoid the likelihood of an urgent call at 3:00 am. We sat cozily together watching TV. Sally, however, became very upset while watching the evening news when she learned of a tragic and distressing event concerning a person she knew. I feared that the shock of the story might stall her progress, but contractions continued to pick up and by 11:00 pm they were coming every three to five minutes. We tried more massage and other stimulating methods to bring labor on, but the contractions doggedly continued to be relatively mild and short. I was looking for more intense contractions of at least a full minute in duration – intense sensations that would require every bit of Sally's attention. Given the current situation, however, I soon suggested that we all try and get some rest. With that, my welcoming hosts showed me to a delightful guest room while they adjourned to their bedroom. Sally's contractions, unfortunately, were too much to be ignored and she was unable to fall asleep. Bill and I managed some catnaps and at 1:30 am I heard movement. They were up again.

We began to circle the downstairs kitchen and dining room area. The contractions became stronger and closer together when Sally kept moving. Despite her fatigue, she bravely paced the circuit a hundred times, stopping to lean over a chair or hang onto Bill each time she had a contraction. Bill studiously timed each surge and would always ask her when it was over. Her reply each time was, "I think it's over, basically." We listened to Bob Marley, chatted to the cats who were bemused by our weird behavior and steadily worked through each contraction. After nearly four hours of walking, the contractions were becoming more intense and I was hopeful that perhaps some changes were occurring. At 5:30 am on Tuesday morning, we left for Plympton Medical Center in two cars – myself following closely through unknown territory and a little fearful of losing them at a red light! Fortunately, we had beaten the rush hour so the roads were quiet.

We arrived at the hospital just before 6:00 am and let ourselves in through the Emergency entrance. We were greeted by Heidi and Carol and began to settle in to Room 429. First, there was a computer glitch so the dozens of apparently irrelevant questions that the nurse had to ask Sally took a while to get completed. Finally, at 6:40 am the big moment had arrived. It was time for Heidi to examine Sally and see what progress she'd made. We waited for the news with baited breath. The baby's head was very low (which indicated a potentially fast pushing stage later on) but the cervix was still in the posterior position and needed to come forward. Furthermore, Sally was still only 60% effaced and just 1 to 2 cm dilated.

This was devastating news after 15 hours of regular contractions. Sally was pretty much the same as she had been at her midwife's visit *last week*. Her disappointment, however, was quickly turned into positive energy by the arrival of our new nurse, Miranda. I wanted to give her "best nurse on the unit" award. She was so upbeat and had absolute trust in Sally's ability to birth her baby. It was wonderfully encouraging to be with her and she helped Sally and Bill work beyond the disappointment of the internal exam.

At 7:40 am, Sally was sucking on a Popsicle and we began the endless walking of the corridors waiting for the midwife to come and check her again. A new nurse, Judy, arrived at 8:00 am and announced that Sally was now 2 cm and 100% effaced. Slow but steady progress indeed. Shortly after, Dr. Kitley arrived and explained that she was going to act the role of Sally's midwife that day, as there were no midwives available. She seemed very open to Sally's wishes and I think Sally and Bill felt comfortable knowing that she would be working with them.

Before she left, Judy offered Sally four options:

- Do nothing and keep going with mild, regular contractions that didn't seem to be making a lot of change in the cervix.

- Go home and try to get some rest and wait until things became more intense.

- Have a medication called Dilaudid to enable Sally to sleep and recuperate before active labor set in.

- Use a prostaglandin gel to stimulate the cervix to soften and open more quickly.

Sally opted for a few hours sleep because she was already exhausted after two broken nights, to be followed by the insertion of some gel to get things moving faster. At 8:30 am, the Dilaudid was administered and Sally immediately fell into a deep sleep. Bill and I were offered pull-out beds by Miranda, who was as solicitous of taking care of us as of her patient. Grateful for her kindness, we too rested for a couple of hours. By 11:30 am, the contractions were waking Sally up and Miranda returned to put on some monitor belts in preparation for the gel while Bill and I tidied up the room. At noon, Sally began to feel very nauseous and the Popsicle she'd just eaten would not stay down. She was still having relentless contractions every three minutes and trying to rest between them. Bill went off to get some lunch and a breath of fresh air, and

I stayed with Sally to help her focus on the contractions.

At 1:10 pm, Dr. Kitley came in to administer the gel and check her again. She was 3 cm and 100% effaced – progress, but oh so slow. Sally was obliged to stay in bed for an hour once the gel had been inserted, wearing the blood pressure cuff and monitor belts. It was all very uncomfortable for her, but she never complained and worked hard to allow the contractions to perform their task. Unfortunately, she continued to feel nauseous, probably because of the Dilaudid, and the nurse gave her some Phernergan to help her stop vomiting. It didn't work very well and Sally continued to be assaulted with feelings of nausea for many hours, making her contractions even harder to cope with.

At 2:30 pm, Sally was able to start moving around, so we tried kneeling over the birth ball on the bed and sitting in the rocking chair for a while. The contractions were becoming more intense now and Sally was working really well with them. Bill never left her side and talked through each surge with her, helping her remain focused and as relaxed as possible. As contractions grew stronger, Sally decided it was time to move into the Jacuzzi, and by 3:30 pm she was lying in the warm water with the loud jets massaging her back and legs. Bill maintained close eye contact with her through each contraction as they grew more intense. He was full of encouragement and praise. Sally began to talk about wanting some other form of pain relief as active labor swooped over her exhausted body and challenged her ability to work with the contractions.

Our new nurse, Pam, helped Sally get out of the Jacuzzi at 4:15 pm and we hobbled back to our room. Pam checked her and announced she was 7 cm dilated! Only 3 cm left to go and those last three can go really fast. Sally and Bill were thrilled with the news but Sally still felt she needed some source of help to get her through. Dr. Kitley was called in to discuss pain relief strategies. Meanwhile, Bill and Sally were in their own world, working in perfect harmony as Bill talked her through each contraction, keeping her focused on the task ahead. At 4:45 pm, Sally was given some Stadol to take the edge off the pain and help her relax some more. She fell into an exhausted sleep immediately, and slept for an hour. By 5:30 pm she was beginning to stir with each contraction, although she still slept between them. Bill took advantage of the hiatus to make some phone calls outside and I sat quietly next to Sally offering her encouragement while she stirred restlessly during the contractions in a half sleep.

By 6:30 pm, the Stadol was completely wearing off and Sally was moaning during contractions, squeezing Bill's hand very tightly. At 6:45 pm, Dr. Kitley returned and checked Sally and broke her waters while doing so. To our utter dismay, she found that Sally was only 5 cm! Pam's 7 cm must have been a very generous and inaccurate estimate. The disappointment in the room was palpable.

Given that Sally still had another 5 cm to dilate, she decided that her best option was to take an epidural so that she could sleep properly without pain. Pitocin would then be administered, which causes the uterus to contract more strongly, and ideally she would open up to 10 cm in a few hours whilst in blissful slumber. She could then wake up refreshed and strong, ready to push her baby out.

Dr. Waters, the anesthesiologist arrived and preparations for the epidural got under-way. I left the room and kept Sally's sister company outside. It seemed that the proce-dure was taking an awfully long time. Sure enough, due to Sally's scoliosis, Dr. Waters was having trouble inserting the epidural in the space between the membranes of the spinal column. She ended up calling a second anesthesiologist and after several attempts, they finally managed to set the epidural up by 8:30 pm. Unfortunately, pain relief was only partial and Sally's dream of "rest and dilate" flew out of the window. At 9:00 pm, Dr. Waters returned to add more medication but Sally was still far from pain free. At 9:30 pm, the Pitocin was started despite Sally's discomfort.

Sally was exhausted and in serious pain despite the epidural and it was at this point that I noticed Bill really stepping up to his task. From somewhere, he found renewed energy and tirelessly worked with Sally during each contraction to keep her on track, never letting her give up. I watched and marveled as his devotion and love for her worked the miracle of keeping her going during this incredibly challenging time. At 11:15 pm, the contractions were getting really intense and Sally was running a slight fever which is not unusual when you have an epidural. Dr. Kitley returned to check her and we all kept our fingers crossed. She was 7 – 8 cm and the baby had turned into a favorable position for delivery! At last, Sally was making real, palpable progress. At the same time, she was becoming more and more exhausted. It was perfectly apparent that Bill's energy and encouragement were keeping her going.

Dr. Waters returned at 11:50 pm to try another epidural as Sally was having so much pain on her left side during the contractions. By 12:15 am, Sally seemed to be getting more relief from the second epidural, but it was by no means 100%. Her pain level descended down to a #5 – fairly uncomfortable. Carol, our nurse, came in to check her at 1:15 am and announced she was 7 cm. – yet another blow to our morale. However, given Sally's exhausted condition and the fact that she and Bill were so wrapped up in the intensity of labor, I'm not sure she was really focusing on those numbers. At 1:45 am Dr. Kitley returned and announced Sally was 10 cm and ready to push! Had she dilated 3 cm in 30 minutes, or was Carol's reading inaccurate? We shall never know.

From somewhere deep in her body, Sally found the energy to start pushing with each contraction at 1:46 am. After a couple of contractions and some detailed in-structions from Dr. Kitley and Carol, Sally began pushing like a pro and the baby slid down the birth canal in a mere 45 minutes, which is very fast for a first time Mom. At last, Sally was being rewarded with a speedy part of labor after nearly forty-eight hours of painfully slow progress.

By 2:30 am, we could see Timothy's head appearing during the pushing. Bill's face was a picture of amazement and joy as he supported Sally's leg and energized her with tireless encouragement. At 2:39 am on Wednesday morning, Timothy was finally de-livered – a fabulous 8½lbs boy, 22 inches long and perfect in every way. Sally's relief was infectious and the room exploded with joy and laughter as Bill cut the umbilical cord. Sally had a small tear that needed to be stitched once the placenta was deliv-ered. Meanwhile, Bill crooned over his newborn son and took photos. It took Bill about half a second to fall head over heels in love for the second time in his life! Sally attempted to breastfeed and Timothy sucked lustily.

These Slow to Start Labors are so hard to cope with. Coupled with the very unusual scenario of an epidural not working properly, Sally and Bill were submitted to a long, hard and challenging labor. But in spite of all the difficulties and repeated setbacks, they never gave up or became despondent. Bill's unwavering support helped Sally through the hardest times, and it was such a joy to watch them work together in perfect harmony.

JAMIE'S BIRTH

From time to time, we all have "one of those days," when it seems that if anything can go wrong…it will. It would have been just another one of those days for Linda, but alas, on this particular day, she was also scheduled to give birth. Now…not to worry. Thankfully, everything turned out just fine. All's well that ends well, as they say. But what a day it was, for this courageous woman and her new family of three.

Linda had a doctor's appointment on Friday afternoon, February 6th, to discuss the results of the ultrasound she'd had that morning and to undergo the usual thirty-eight week prenatal check up. The ultrasound showed a baby whose size was somewhat small for the standard gestation benchmark dates. Linda's doctor suspected that this could be due to her persistent high blood pressure, which perhaps, was preventing normal blood flow through the placenta. In turn, it was possible that the baby was no longer receiving nutrition to grow at a steady pace. With the high blood pressure and small baby in mind, Dr. Chessman strongly suggested that Linda go in to the hospital that very evening, where Cervidil would be administered in preparation for an induction the following morning. Cervidil softens the cervix and prepares it for dilation. This unexpected news led to a busy and flustered afternoon with much organizing and telephoning on Linda's part.

She and husband Art set out for Haytor hospital at 6:00 pm and settled in to Room 437 – where unbeknownst to them, an avalanche of mishaps was poised for its raucous, rumbling slide. The mountain started to move at some point in the evening, when their toilet flooded and threatened to spill over into the room. With that unpleasant possibility, they were hastily moved next door to Room 438 at the end of the corridor. Apparently, a total of three toilets overflowed that evening in the hospital, prompting multiple migrations of patients up and down the hallway. Given the general state of interruption, the Cervidil was not administered to Linda until 8 pm. This consistent delay in action, we soon learned, turned out to be the norm – known as "hospital time." I called at 8:15 pm and Linda was lying down, looking forward to getting something to eat and then sleeping through the night in preparation for the induction at 8:00 am the next morning.

At around midnight, after Art had gone home to get some sleep, Linda's waters broke. She soon began to throw up her dinner – so violently, in fact, that the Cervidil fell out from the effects of her retching. So much for a good night's sleep! On top of this, she began having contractions almost immediately. These were full-blown contractions, two to three minutes apart – none of the slow, gentle, build-up-to-labor-contractions, which the majority of first time moms experience. Taken off guard by her body's sudden upheaval, Linda called me at 1:00 am, requesting my support. She made a conscious decision not to phone Art, as she wanted him to get some much-needed rest during these early hours of labor. I arrived at 1:45 am and found Linda working hard through her contractions, which were persistently regular and quite uncomfortable. Kelly, our delightful nurse for the night, had Dr. Chessman on the phone. He requested a progress report, which for Linda, meant the further discomfort of undergoing a vaginal exam.

At 2:00 am Kelly announced that Linda was 1 cm dilated and her cervix was "super soft" and thin, which meant that further dilation could potentially occur quickly. Dr. Chessman's phone response was to "wait and see," the hope being that Linda would continue on this labor path and Pitocin induction the following morning would be redundant. Next on the list of *Exciting Things That Can Happen to You in Labor*: Linda threw up excessively; she began shaking uncontrollably; contractions became *very* intense every two minutes. The "avalanche," was picking up speed.

It was extremely uncomfortable for her to lie down in any position on the bed and so despite her growing fatigue, Linda spent the next two hours either sitting on the Birth Ball or in the rocking chair between contractions. During each contraction, every two minutes, she would heave herself up and pace the room, up and down, up and down, like a tiger in a cage. Movement seemed to be the only thing that alleviated the pain of the contractions.

Occasionally, she would stop, lean over something and sway rhythmically from side to side. It is extraordinary to see a woman's inner body wisdom come to light during labor as she finds her very own unique and personal path to coping with the intense sensations of the birthing process. I watched in awe as Linda developed her own coping ritual with every contraction. I soothed her with my voice and comforting presence and was careful not to interfere with her birthing ritual.

By 4:00 am however, Linda was becoming exhausted and so she managed to stay seated in the rocking chair during contractions and maintain movement by rocking vigorously. By so doing, she didn't have to keep heaving herself back onto her feet and she was able to sink into a light doze in the brief respite between contractions, her head lolling to one side and her eyes closed. She also made a long visit to the bathroom, where sitting on the toilet proved to be another viable option and I listened to her moaning gently as each contraction surged through her.

At 4:30 am contractions were too intense to sit through, whether on the toilet or in the rocking chair and we tried other ideas such as kneeling on all fours. Linda was very good-natured about experimenting with alternatives, but ended up returning to movement as her only option. Once again, she took up the ritual of pacing the room like a caged tiger during contractions, then resting in the rocking chair between them.

At 6:00 am Kelly checked Linda again. She was 3½ cm dilated and the baby had moved down 2 cm from -3 to -1 station. (He needed to go from -4 through 0 to +4 station in order to see the light of day.) This was slow but steady progress. In four hours of intense labor Linda had dilated 2 cm and the baby had descended 2 cm. If Linda had not been so exhausted, this news would have been encouraging, as it is considered normal progress for a first time Mom.

Given her lack of sleep and food, and the assumption that she had at least another six hours of this dilation stage with intense contractions every two minutes, Linda was beginning to realize that she needed to get some sleep. We discussed pain medication options and Linda decided that having an epidural was her best choice, as it would allow her to get some desperately needed rest while her body continued to labor.

At 6:45 am a nurse came in to start the IV and give her a bag of fluid. This additional hydration was a preventative measure, intended to counterbalance the epidural anesthetic, which can sometimes cause a drop in blood pressure. (The epidural did indeed cause a drop in Linda's blood pressure, which was actually a good thing in her case.) At 7:00 am Kelly announced that Dr. Daniel Widner, the anesthesiologist, was on his way. At 7:15 am, our new nurse Fran arrived to set up continuous monitoring for Linda, a necessary precursor to the epidural.

Fran was loud and upbeat, sometimes to the point of being irritating. (Art later likened her to a cheerleader, which was very apt, especially later, during the push-ing stage!) Once again, "hospital time" reared its ugly head and Linda had to wait another forty-five minutes for Dr. Widner to finally arrive to place the epidural. Fran was overwhelmed by having to take care of several laboring women at once, so Alison, another much quieter nurse came in to help out with the epidural. The administration went smoothly and by 8:05 am, Linda was relaxed and comfortable and ready to fall asleep.

Dr. Chessman came in to see us and suggested some pitocin to keep the labor going, as labor can sometimes stall with the use of an epidural. At 8:15 am, Linda was fast asleep listening to some relaxing music on her IPod. Art arrived at about 8:30 am and Linda woke briefly to recount the night's adventures to him. She then fell back to sleep.

The morning passed quietly enough with the usual hospital interruptions: vital signs being checked; catheters being inserted; and Fran disrupting the calm. But for the most part Linda slept, I dozed in the armchair and Art waited patiently for labor to unfold. By 11:30 am, the contractions were clearly showing up as being very strong on the monitor due to the use of Pitocin and the baby was beginning to show some signs of distress during them. By "distress," I mean that the baby's heart rate slowed down. Given this situation, Linda was frequently asked to change positions in order to accommodate her baby.

These types of heart "decels" during contractions are fairly commonly detected when continuous monitoring is used. They are not a cause for serious concern, provided that the baby's heart rate recuperates between contractions. Heart deceleration can be due to positioning, cord compression or the baby's head being compressed as he moves down the birth canal. Fran checked Linda and to our delight announced that she was now 7 to 8 cm dilated and 90% effaced with the baby still at -1 station.

One hour later at 12:30 pm, Dr. Chessman came in and checked Linda again. She was now 9½ cm dilated and the baby had moved down to 0 station. Due to the continuing heart decels, he suggested backing off on the Pitocin, as the labor was clearly progressing at a good speed. Fran recommended passive descent rather than active pushing at this stage. This meant allowing the contractions to move the baby down further into the birth canal before actively pushing. So, for another hour Linda continued to rest while all the time her body was working hard to birth her baby.

At 1:30 pm, Linda appeared to be going through the transition phase as she began to shake violently. Fran gave her some oxygen to counteract the baby's heart decels, which seemed to do the trick. At 1:45 pm Dr. Chessman checked her again and announced that she was fully dilated and the baby had moved down to +1 station. It was time to start pushing.

To our great relief, our cheerleading nurse was too occupied in Room 437 (I guess the plumber must have come and gone) so Melissa came in to help us with the pushing stage. In spite of Fran's experience and good intentions, it must be said that Melissa's calmer, quieter demeanor suited us better. Our relief was short-lived, however, as Fran could not resist returning to us for the birth. During those last fifteen minutes of pushing, while Linda and Art were focusing on the incredible journey their baby was taking, Fran and Melissa seemed obsessed by the wondrous beauty of Linda's gown (with matching robe) that she had bought especially for the birth. This gown, in fact, had caused quite a commotion throughout the day, as she enjoyed wearing it despite the nurses' constant warnings that it would get dirty! Poor Linda. It should have been obvious that this was what she had bought it for, but the nursing staff just didn't get it. Their constant chatter was irritating to Linda and Art who were so focused on birthing their baby.

Linda learned how to push effectively within a couple of contractions. This is no easy feat when an epidural is removing most sensation from the waist down. She began pushing shortly before 2:00 pm and within fifteen minutes we could spy the top of the baby's head during a contraction. Art stayed by her head and offered her constant encouragement. Melissa and I helped her by supporting a leg while she pushed. Less than an hour later, at 2:47 pm, Jamie slipped out into the world.

The cord was wrapped once around his neck, as is the case in about 30% of babies, and Dr. Chessman cut it immediately rather than trying to lift it over his head. Jamie had some difficulties getting his breathing started and after a microsecond of being placed on Linda's belly, he was whisked off to the baby warmer a couple of feet away. There, several nurses and doctors busied themselves quietly and efficiently to get him breathing. I must say it was terrifying for Linda, Art and me. Each second we waited for him to breathe seemed like an eternity. After three minutes of urgent care by the medical team, little Jamie began to pink up and tension in the room palpably diminished. By now a neonatology doctor was taking care of him and examined him carefully. He announced that Jamie looked fine and there should be no lasting repercussions to his initial breathing problem.

Meanwhile, Dr. Chessman, having first helped out with Jamie, had now returned to Linda and was struggling to deliver the placenta. Sweat began to pour down his brow as he pulled aggressively on the umbilical cord with each contraction, to no avail. Linda was preoccupied with Jamie's situation and did not notice the look of consternation on Melissa and Dr. Chessman's face. After thirty-five minutes of tugging, Dr. Chessman announced that Linda would have to go into the Operating Room and have the placenta manually removed under a short-lasting general anesthetic. She was able to briefly hold Jamie for five minutes before he was taken to the nursery for close observation.

At 3:45 pm we wheeled Linda down the corridor to the Operating Room and she disappeared from my sight for the first time in fifteen hours. I felt desolate – this is was not how birth was meant to be. Jamie and Art spent the next hour in the nursery with a nurse whose attitude contributed to the ever-growing "snowball" of this day's frustrations. She appeared to show no sensitivity or compassion towards Art, who was stressed and frightened by the unexpected turn of events. It must have been a very difficult time for him and I longed to be able to go into the nursery to comfort him. All I could do was look through the window and watch him gently caress his son, who responded by remaining calm and content.

Finally, at 4:30 pm, they brought Linda back into the room and announced that the procedure had been successful. Dr. Chessman commented that the placenta had been somewhat calcified, which meant that it probably was no longer 100% efficient in its job. This would have likely accounted for the initial concerns that were discovered via the ultrasound. Linda was groggy but in amazingly good spirits. We waited for the nursery nurses to finish their observation of Jamie and bathe him. In yet *another* frustrating moment, Art came in and told us that they would not allow Jamie to return to Linda until his breathing had slowed down. The three of us sat in complete silence. I felt *so* upset. If only they would bring Jamie to be with his mom. Surely, I thought, this was the best way to stabilize his breathing. But I knew that the rules and regulations and liability issues of the nursery were written in stone and I held my thoughts to myself.

Linda was understandably upset because she still hadn't gotten to hold her son for more than a second. Melissa called the nursery nurse in, who begrudgingly agreed to allow him in for twenty minutes at Linda and Art's insistence. After twenty minutes he would have to return to the nursery for a final check on his vital signs and blood sugar. Finally, at 5:00 pm, Linda was able to hold her precious baby in her arms. He was too sleepy to want to nurse by this time, but oh the joy of nuzzling his mother's breast, of smelling her and hearing her voice at last. Twenty sweet minutes together and then he and his dad returned for their final stint in the nursery.

Linda and I sat quietly in her room waiting for them to return. Melissa busied herself taking care of Linda and we both dozed, trying to assimilate all that had happened in the last three hours. Within an hour Jamie was pronounced stable on all fronts and came back in to us after his bath and final check up. This time, he was wide-awake and latched on immediately to Linda's breast. He fed lustily for thirty solid minutes! The look of pure joy on Linda and Art's faces made every single tough minute fade into the background of my mind. It was sad that this moment had not occurred at 2:47 pm, but at last it was happening now and all was well. After his long and satisfying feeding, Jamie was held lovingly in his father's arms for the first time. I left the new family alone to enjoy these precious first moments of being together in peace and quiet at last.

"Her body was telling her that she needed to keep moving, but each time she changed position the monitor would lose its tracing."

THE SOMEWHAT PRECIPITOUS ARRIVAL OF KATIE EATON

I haven't been on a rollercoaster in years, but I clearly remember what the ride is like (which is why it's been such a long time). First, there's the torturously slow, nerve-racking climb up some long, ridiculously high ramp. You rattle along skyward for what seems like an eternity – the queasiness of your stomach growing in direct proportion to your ascent. And then, just when you begin to think your misery will never end…well, you know what happens. I believe they call it "freefalling," which to put it mildly, stands in stark contrast to your long, slow climb. Such was the experience of Jenny, who gave birth on a rollercoaster – figuratively speaking, of course.

Jenny had not been feeling at all well on April 14th. "*Had not been feeling well*" was a relative term, considering she had not been feeling well throughout her entire pregnancy. April 14th was simply a little worse than the previous 256 days. Kevin had not wanted her to be driving alone, so her mom had come that morning to drive Jenny and three year old Ned to school. Jenny had been driven back home and curled up on the sofa for the rest of the day. I visited her briefly in the afternoon, and she certainly did look unhappy. She was feeling lots of pressure, some cramping and was as nauseous as she had been over the previous eight and a half months. The following morning, on April 15th, she noticed some fluid and realized that her waters might have broken. It was not the big gush like last time with Ned, but a trickle, which indicated a nick in the bag rather than a fully blown tear.

At around noon, Kevin, Ned and Jenny headed off to the doctor's office where she was checked and the doctor confirmed that her waters had indeed broken. Given that Jenny, like 40% of all healthy women, was Group B positive (GBS+), the doctor strongly recommended that she head over to the hospital even though she was not yet in labor. This was because it is recommended that women who are GBS+ be given antibiotics as a prophylactic, to avoid passing infection on to their infants during the birthing process.

First, Kevin and Jenny needed to organize childcare for Ned, so their friend and babysitter Sally took him temporarily, until Grandma could come and take over. Kevin and

Jenny arrived at St. Marks in New Wolton at about 2:00 pm and were admitted to Room 4. They were treated to a very pleasant view, lovely green walls and a matching green gown for Jenny to wear – a definite upgrade since Ned's arrival three years previously. Lily was slated to be their nurse until 7:00 pm and she enhanced the already-positive atmosphere with her friendly and cheerful demeanor.

Unfortunately, nobody was very successful at attempting to insert the IV into the back of Jenny's hand. It was only after much painful prodding and poking, and attempts by two different nurses, that an IV line was finally inserted successfully. In the middle of the afternoon, Dr. Porto arrived to examine Jenny and discuss options. Jenny was 1 cm dilated and 50% effaced, but not yet in established labor. Because her waters had broken, she was on a timeline to have her baby within about twenty-four hours, so something had to be done to get the labor started. Dr. Porto suggested inserting a suppository of Cytotec into the birth canal every four hours for two or three doses and then Pitocin after that if necessary. It sounded like we were in for the long haul.

At 4:00 pm the first dose of Cytotec was inserted and Jenny was told to lie still for an hour while the suppository dissolved. She was not yet experiencing strong contractions, so it was not too uncomfortable to lie on the bed. When I arrived at 6:15 pm the contractions had begun to pick up a little, but Jenny still had a big smile on her face and was talking normally between them. By now, the Cytotec had dissolved so she was able to move around again. Jenny tried to get as comfortable as possible and made the best of the situation, given all the paraphernalia that she was hooked up to (two monitor belts, the blood pressure cuff, and the IV line in her hand). She found that the most comfortable position was standing, as this took the pressure off her back. So she put her arms around Kevin's neck and they swayed together, performing a 6th Grade (Kevin's interpretation) or 4th Grade (Jenny's interpretation) dance routine.

Kevin started to show us what an 8th Grade dance routine might look like, but another contraction came and we were back to the serious work of having a baby before his hands could wander any farther! A hot pack on her back gave her some relief from the persistent back pain, but after half an hour or so, Jenny began to feel a little tired and tried sitting on the edge of the bed. There, she leaned forward onto Kevin's chest while I applied pressure and heat to her lower back. Moaning gently through each contraction, she coped brilliantly as the pace of her labor began to quicken. Small talk died out in the room.

Things really started to pick up at about 7:30 pm when Jenny felt a gush of fluid. The fore waters had broken, which meant that the baby's head would now move down onto her cervix. As a result, she would feel much more pressure and her contractions would become stronger, longer and closer together. These changes in her labor were almost immediate and I began to think there would be no need for a second dose of Cytotec. It was at this time that Kevin suggested we try using the TENS unit for pain relief. TENS stands for Transcutaneous Electrical Nerve Stimulation and consists of four electrodes placed strategically on the back. The electrodes pulsate gently, thereby distracting the mother from the sensation of the contractions. TENS units are commonly used in maternity hospitals in Canada, Australia and the UK. Given that the use of the TENS in labor is unknown at St. Marks' hospital, I recommended we first get permission from Dr. Porto. Jenny had gotten her own consent form but Dr. Porto was not aware of that. Lily went off to find her and Jenny continued working hard with her labor.

Our new nurse, Sarah – who looked like she should be at one of those 8th grade dances Kevin had been talking about – replaced Lily. Sarah truly appeared to be about fourteen, which was no fault of her own. But, she also seemed incapable of smiling. It wasn't that she was mean or unpleasant; she just wasn't warm or friendly. I must say this was a real let-down after our enjoyable experience with Lily. What an enormous difference a smile can make!

At about 8:30 pm, Dr. Porto came in to discuss the option of using the TENS unit. After reading the information, and after many quizzical looks, she agreed to allow Jenny to use the TENS, which I quickly applied to her back. Unfortunately, the long wait meant that we had started it a little too late. The contractions were already strong, so its effectiveness was diminished. Jenny said the tingling sensation helped her to relax between contractions, however she barely noticed it *during* the contractions.

The next hour was surreal. Jenny's labor picked up to lightening speed. She moaned and cried through the contractions, clinging to Kevin and not wanting him to leave her sight. At 8:53 pm, during a particularly challenging contraction, she actually bit him on the left breast. Perhaps she was trying to stop herself from crying out, or perhaps she was allowing Kevin just a glimmer of what it feels like to birth a baby! Kevin, however, was stalwart in his loving support of Jenny — holding her tight, encouraging her, reassuring her and wiping the hair from her face. (Note: For baby number three, bring a hair band.) During this time, the optimum position for Jenny seemed to be kneeling on the bed over the birth ball. Unfortunately, the fetal heart monitor did not want to stay in position when she was configured like this. Sullen Sarah repeatedly came in and demanded that she change position.

Just before 9:00 pm, Dr. Porto returned to examine Jenny again. Being told she had to lie on her back for the examination was really hard for her to hear. (Jenny could only manage her pain by sitting upright, getting on all fours, or standing up.) This already difficult situation was made worse by Sarah, who — with a voice entirely void of compassion — bluntly stated, "You have to do this." (I'm pretty sure that Sarah has not had a baby yet. It will be interesting to see how her manner changes when and if she does.) With extreme difficulty, Jenny maneuvered herself onto her back and Dr. Porto checked her. The doctor announced that Jenny was 4 to 5 cm dilated, 100% effaced and the baby was at -1 station. This was good progress, but given the intensity of Jenny's contractions, we were all expecting and hoping for a bigger number. (In order for the baby to pass through the birth canal, the cervix has to thin out from 0 to 100%, to open from 0 to 10 cm and the baby has to move down from -4 through 0 to +4 station.) Kevin and I had about 2:30 am in our minds as the likely birthing hour. How wrong we both were!

For the next half an hour, Jenny labored ferociously. Her strength and courage in working with her labor were amazing and awesome to witness. There was no break between contractions and the pain in her back was excruciating as she felt the baby move down. Her body was telling her that she needed to keep moving, but each time she changed position the monitor would lose its tracing. Dr. Porto suggested inserting an internal fetal scalp monitor, which would allow Jenny more freedom of movement than the belt monitors did. At 9:30 pm Dr. Porto once again checked Jenny while applying the fetal scalp monitor and announced that she was now 8 cm dilated and the baby had moved down to +1 station. She had gone from 4 to 8 cm in a record thirty minutes!

The next eight minutes were a blur of activity. Jenny moved onto all fours and immediately announced a very strong urge to push. Leaving her on all fours, Dr. Porto once again checked her and discovered she was fully dilated at 10 cm. There was no stopping her! She had two pushing contractions on all fours while Dr. Porto gowned up and then we got her to move onto her back, ready to birth her baby. One contraction later and we could see the top of the baby's head. There was feverish activity in the room: Kevin handed me the camera while holding Jenny's leg. I unsuccessfully tried to get the mirror into place (so that Jenny could see her baby coming out) while not getting in Dr. Porto's way. Sarah was holding Jenny's other leg while trying to help Dr. Porto get ready for the birth. It was like being in a contest for multi-taskers.

Two more pushes and at 9:38 pm, Katie slipped out into the world. Kevin cut the cord while I, having failed in the mirror department, tried to get some photos – no easy feat when there are several people surrounding the baby. Katie was in perfect shape and happily nuzzled up to her Mom, looking at the world with her beautiful brown eyes. The nurse swaddled her and weighed her. She was 6 lbs. 4oz and 19¾ inches long, a healthy newborn and as cute as a button. Jenny was shaking from the extreme exertion her body had just been through. Kevin held Katie while Dr. Porto delivered the placenta and gave Jenny a couple of stitches to repair a minor tear. Then Kevin and Katie went off to the nursery together for a more thorough check up. Jenny relished in eating a banana and the shaking gradually began to subside.

At 11:00 pm Jenny, Katie, Kevin and I moved across to a luxurious new postpartum suite, Room 425, and settled in. There, *real* food was waiting for her. Unfortunately, it took several attempts with two different microwaves to heat it up. The room was gorgeous, a beautiful environment for Jenny to settle in with her new daughter and recuperate from the whirlwind labor she had just experienced. These fast, precipitous labors are very hard to deal with and Jenny was incredibly strong and brave. With Kevin's constant support and her indomitable courage, they accomplished in *one intense hour*, what often takes ten hours! Thank you Jenny and Kevin, for the honor of being part of this lightening speed labor. You are an incredibly strong couple!

Births by CESAREAN

"The baby was a strong little boy: he grabbed a plastic tube with his little fist and would not let go."

TAMSIN'S BIRTH

There is certainly something to be said for the power of trust. Quiet and childlike, trust, at first glance, might appear to be simple. And it can be simple – when everything seems to be going in our favor; or when the risks are small; or when the outcomes are inconsequential. But when the opposite is true – when nothing seems to be working out; when the odds are stacked against us; when the consequences really do matter – simple trust can seem beyond our reach. As a doula, I am in awe of those I have worked with, who have faced the uncertainties and risks of childbirth and who have conquered their fears and doubts, through the power of trust. Among those I admire, is Tamsin, whose simple trust provided a foundation for her amazing courage and composure.

At 7:30 am, Tamsin and Neil arrived at the admissions desk of the North West Hospital in Thatcham, looking relaxed and happy. A few jokes about the resuscitation (or rather, no resuscitation) clauses in the paperwork she had to sign, and already I was marveling at their ability to remain so calm and collected when major abdominal surgery was only a couple of hours ahead. By 8:00 am, we were able to settle in to Room 431 in the presence of our nurse Kerry. Her main preoccupation throughout the whole day was how often the computer took her away from her true job: one-to-one contact with her patients. Kerry was obviously very frustrated and angry at having to devote herself to a screen rather than to Tamsin and we sympathized with her. I was just glad that Neil and I were here to be with Tamsin – no computers for us today! We also met briefly with Barbara, the baby nurse. Later on, Dr. Samuels, the anesthesiologist, came in to explain all the procedures to us concerning the "spinal" and the surgery. He was very informative and I appreciated his quiet and respectful manner.

For the next two hours we chatted about this and that and I gave Tamsin a foot massage which seemed just right – not too distracting so that she couldn't talk to the nurse and to Neil, but distracting enough to keep her relaxed and calm. I admired her quiet self-confidence. She knew exactly what was going to happen but never once did she allow herself to panic or become anxious. At about nine o'clock we learned that Dr. Eggland, the obstetrician, had to go over to Thatcham General for an emergency cesarean birth. So, with that, our 9:30 am start was going to be pushed back about half an hour. Tamsin took this in her stride and we just continued the foot massage, enjoying lovely piano music in the background. Neil was full of smiles and was being very supportive, showing no signs of stress or anxiety.

At about 10:00 am I did some touch relaxation with Tamsin, who said her shoulders were stiffening up. This led us on to employ other effective relaxation techniques. I read her a countdown relaxation, followed by a rainbow relaxation – a visualization of a baby floating through the colors of the rainbow. She responded so well, concentrating intently on my words, despite all the other things that were going on (like the blood pressure sleeve automatically blowing up on her arm while the nurse was simultaneously asking Neil questions).

Perfect timing…Just as we were about to finish, Dr. Samuels came in and said it was time to go to the operating room and have the spinal. Neil and I had to stay in Room 431 until the spinal was administered and then we would be called. I perceived a fleeting moment of anxiety and fear flash across Tamsin's face as she was wheeled out of the room and away from us. More than anything in the world, I wanted to go with her and hold her hand, but I knew that making that kind of request was breaking operating room etiquette and I needed to watch my P's and Q's if I wanted to work here again!

Neil and I had fifteen minutes alone together, all togged up in our scrubs, which included hats, shoes and masks. We talked briefly about Tamsin slowly coming to terms with not having the vaginal delivery she had dreamed of. I mentioned that this grieving process may take some time, even though she would have a beautiful, healthy baby. Neil understood completely and I knew that he would help her through this loss. Kerry came back and it was time for us to go to the O.R.

The operating room was bright and airy and in fact, rather pleasant, considering it was so surgical. Neil and I were whisked around past the sterile field by Dr. Samuels and given our allotted place on either side of Tamsin's head – Neil choosing the left and I, the right. Quite a prestigious group had assembled in the operating room for this procedure. Also with Neil and me was Steven the technician, Kerry, Dr. Eggland and his colleague Dr. Oldham, Dr. Blair the pediatrician, Dr. Samuels and Paula, another nurse for the baby. Piano music drifted from a boom box and the atmosphere was calm and efficient. Tamsin was coping brilliantly, maintaining her aura of peacefulness. No time was wasted and before we knew it, the sterile drape was raised and the surgery began.

Despite my curiosity regarding the procedure, I was determined to concentrate 100% on Tamsin and carefully watch how she was doing – always ready to calm her and help her remain relaxed. Her self-control, however, was incredible and she spent most of the next ten minutes listening intently to the running commentary given by Neil, as to what was happening on the other side of the drape. Dr. Samuels filled in on a few details, but otherwise, Neil provided the "play-by-play." No fainting fits or ashen face for this father. He was totally absorbed in the birth of his baby, describing each incision and getting visibly more excited as the doctors spied the baby's bottom.

At 10:43 am, a perfect baby was born and it was Neil's privilege to announce that they had another boy! I stood on my tiptoes, peering over the drape as I tried to take a few photos with the cord still attached. The baby was covered in vernix and started to cry almost immediately – a lusty, energetic cry, which left us in no doubt that Tamsin and Neil had created a wonderful, healthy baby. The baby was shown briefly to Tamsin and was then taken over to the warmer to be checked. As in all cesarean births, there were one or two things that needed to be done which are fairly routine: he had to be given a little oxygen from an oxygen mask; he had to have a tube inserted into his throat to remove any fluid that might have accumulated. I instinctively wanted to stay next to Tamsin, but she was keen to have some photos of her newborn, and seemed to be thriving on the excitement of the birth of her baby. She was not in need of any special doula care at that point, so I went over to the baby with Neil and took lots of pictures for them. All this time, Dr. Blair was talking to Neil and explaining all sorts of things to him, while reassuring him that the baby was fine. His Apgars were 8 and 9 – excellent scores for a cesarean birth.

The baby was a strong little boy: he grabbed a plastic tube with his little fist and would not let go. Dr. Blair had to gently prize open his tiny fingers in order to reclaim his plastic tube! Fortunately, Tamsin could see the baby from where she was lying. She was already half-way to being sewn up and it was so wonderful to see her happy, smiling face. What a brave lady to have undergone such an experience for her baby, and to have kept smiling all the way through. Neil held the baby, tightly wrapped in his blankets, eyes still closed because of the bright lights, and took him to Tamsin for a few minutes so that she might touch him and feel his soft skin on her face. I hoped the photo of the three of them together for the first time would come out well – it was such a beautiful picture and I would always treasure it in my memory.

At 11:00 a.m., Neil went back to the room with his newborn son while I stayed with Tamsin who was still being sewn up. She was chatting to Dr. Eggland and we all joked about names – the most popular idea being "Frank Breech Clapham!" Once again, I was full of admiration for her composure and her ability to deal so well with such a stressful situation and make it into the wondrous event that it was.

By 11:15 am she was all ready to return to her room and her baby. We rolled her off the operating bed with ease and wheeled her back to Room 431. The baby had been weighed and measured by now and he was 7 lbs and 10oz – much heavier than most of us would have predicted. He was 20½ inches long; his chest was 12½ inches and his head 14 inches in circumference. Quite a lad! Tamsin wanted to feed him as soon as possible and he had a short suckle though he seemed to be more interested in sleeping right then. I saw that Neil was jubilant holding his new son and Tamsin was full of excitement despite the surgery she had just undergone. Neil phoned their son Liam and told him that he could come and visit his new sibling. As part of the fun, he didn't tell him whether he had a brother or a sister! A quarter of an hour later, Liam and his babysitter, Kay, arrived downstairs and I took them up to the room. Liam was so excited and it was a precious moment to watch him enter the room and see his little brother for the first time. Tamsin allowed him to discover the sex of the baby for himself. His exclamation, "it's a boy!" was so full of joy and awe. What a wonderful big brother he would be.

Tamsin's close friend, Rose, arrived at about noon, and Neil and Liam went off downstairs to get some lunch. By now Tamsin was beginning to feel really tired and I was anxious that she should soon be able to rest for a few hours. Rose and I watched over the baby while he had his eye drops and Vitamin K shot in the thigh. He only woke momentarily and then drifted off back to a peaceful sleep. Kerry was worried that his blood sugar might be low, as he was a bit jittery, but a blood test proved this not to be the case, so bottles of sugar water and formula could be avoided.

It was bath time, so I went downstairs to fetch dad and big brother who had just finished lunch. We all watched as he was gently washed with warm water (no soap as requested by Tamsin – a first for Kerry) and had his hair shampooed, which he seemed to like. Kerry took obvious pleasure in trying various hairstyles on him. I think she was more into this than his mom and dad were, but they decided eventually on a side parting on the left! Quite dapper!

It was time for Rose to go home and put the placenta in her deep freeze (to be planted under a tree at some future date) and time for baby to try another feeding. He still seemed too tired to be really bothered about food, but no matter, there was plenty of time for him to get hungry before the day was out. I reassured Tamsin that he would manage just fine on his own reserves for a few hours. Tamsin was looking really tired at that point and I felt that I should leave. I hoped that she would manage to take a nap. It was hard to leave this lovely family, who had done such a fantastic job bringing their new baby into the world. I wished I could have stayed all day and watch all of them getting to know their new baby.

"They had only minutes to adjust to the reality that Naomi was about to have major abdominal surgery and give birth to her baby."

MARCEL'S BIRTH

The other day, I found myself standing in a long line at the DMV. Given the venue, I was pleasantly surprised to find that we snaked along at a fairly reasonable pace. That all changed when the man in front of me got to the counter. There, the clerk informed him that he was missing some particular document, and that he would need to retrieve it and get back in line. Apparently, this proved to be totally insurmountable for him and he embarked on a tantrum that would have impressed even the most seasoned two-year-old. As pathetic as his behavior was, he caused me to think of those who live their lives on the other end of the character spectrum. People who possess inner wisdom and maturity, who are able to rise above their circumstances and remain poised in the face of frustrating – even fearful – situations. People like Naomi and Frank.

Naomi began having mild contractions on Friday, November 5th, at around 9:00 am. These became more regular in the afternoon, and by evening they were coming every five to ten minutes. She called me mid-evening to bring me up to speed on her condition. Our conversation had just begun, when she stopped talking and focused in silence on a contraction. She then resumed chatting happily until the next contraction rose within her. I saw this as a positive indication that labor was progressing, but also, that it was probably still in the early stages.

She and Frank were both coping well and worked in harmony to breathe and relax through each contraction. Naomi spent half the night in a glider chair in the baby's room and the other half in a chair in the bedroom. All the while, Frank patiently logged the time and duration of every contraction. Throughout the night, they listened to a hypnobirthing CD. Its soothing music and serene messages helped Naomi stay calm and composed. The couple continued in this manner all night long, until the early hours of Saturday, when they decided that it was time to go to Whitehaven Hospital.

They arrived at Whitehaven at 7:30 am and were disappointed to find that both their doctors were out on vacation. This left them with a Dr. Robert Sands, who was clearly not sympathetic to their birth choices. He made this very clear from the beginning, but agreed to "leave them alone" unless necessity arose. To his credit, he stuck to his word. Upon their arrival, Naomi and Frank were taken care of by RN's Judy and Maggie. Judy warmed to us as she came to realize that Naomi and Frank were not "difficult clients"; they simply wanted their birth preferences respected whenever possible. Judy checked Naomi who was found to be 5 cm dilated and 90% effaced with the baby lying nice and low in the pelvis. This was good news. Those twenty-four hours of regular contractions had been effective.

At 9:00 am, a nurse came to insert a Heplock in Naomi's arm. A Heplock is an IV port that allows an IV line to be connected immediately in the event of an emergency. Naomi was very stalwart as the nurse poked her repeatedly, without success. Finally the anesthesiologist was called in and with his superior equipment, managed to find a vein that would work. It must have been unpleasant for Naomi to deal with this, while at the same time, experiencing contractions.

At 10:00 am Naomi decided to move into the whirlpool tub at the end of the corridor, to ease her pain and help her to relax. We shuffled down the hallway and she sank into the warm water. The contractions seemed to pick up a little, which was a good sign and the warm water definitely helped her to relax and rest better between them. Her entire body began to shake uncontrollably during the contractions, probably due to exhaustion. Understandably, this was upsetting to Naomi and Judy brought her a warmed towel to help ease the shaking. She had been working hard for twenty-four hours already and had taken little food. An hour later, she decided to leave the tub.

She returned to her room where Judy insisted on monitoring her as much as possible – at the very least, for twenty minutes every hour. All morning Naomi and Frank worked remarkably well with the contractions. Naomi would do a rhythmic "hee hee ho" breathing throughout the contraction, while Frank held her and encouraged her. I discreetly conducted the rhythm with my hand to help her keep on track. She was coping beautifully.

At 1:15 pm, Judy checked Naomi and she was now 7 to 8 cm dilated with the baby very low at 0 station. (The baby has to descend from -4 to +4 station during labor.) This was slow but steady progress and Naomi and Frank were pleased and relieved to know that they were on the right track. At this point, Naomi decided to brush her teeth – an amazing feat when in hard, active labor!

The afternoon progressed and we continued the work of labor. Every twenty minutes or so, Naomi would change positions to encourage the baby to rotate and move down. She was willing to try any suggestions to help her labor progress and we went through the entire list of possible configurations: squatting; kneeling over the birth ball; standing; pelvic rocking and walking. Through all of this, she never complained or became downhearted. For Naomi, the most comfortable position (a relative term at this point) was sitting on the chair. She knew, however, that sitting still was not optimal, so she would force herself, despite her fatigue, to regularly get up and move around.

Naomi was amazing and never lost her smile between contractions. Frank regularly presented her with vivid green popsicles in order to give her a little energy with some sugar. Clearly, lime green was not Naomi's choice of flavor, but she maintained her sense of humor and the ubiquitous green popsicles always brought a smile to her weary face. Throughout the labor I reminded Naomi to drink water for the sake of staying hydrated and keeping her energy up.

At 3:00 pm in the afternoon Judy left us and her replacement, Zaid arrived. Zaid was willing to leave us to our work, but insisted on checking Naomi at 5:00 pm. With that examination, Naomi was found to *still* be 8 cm dilated. This was disappointing news, as she had been working so hard all afternoon. At 5:30 pm, after some more monitoring, we started walking the corridors. Everyone was hopeful that some more active movement might help her reach full dilation. Sure enough, as soon as Naomi began pacing the corridors, the contractions came much stronger and closer together. This was exactly what we had hoped for, but the increased pain made mobility a real challenge. Undaunted, Naomi stuck to her plan and continued to walk.

Dr. Sands returned at 6:30 pm. He stomped into our quiet, peaceful room, with its gentle, soothing music – and the atmosphere immediately changed. His message was clear: he had respected Naomi's birth preferences all day, but now it was time for him to take over. She had been at 8 cm for too long and he suggested rupturing her membranes to see what was going on. Given the circumstances (no change all afternoon), this was sound and sensible advice – but his delivery was that of an NFL coach whose team was losing. He was rude and brutal. This was his way of dealing with working under pressure and getting his patients to do what was needed.

Remarkably, Naomi and Frank were not ruffled and after a few minutes they agreed to the intervention. Dr. Sands checked her and she was still at 8 cm with a cervix that was beginning to swell with all the pressure from the baby's head. This, disturbingly, was counterproductive to dilation. Furthermore, upon breaking the bag, he noticed some blood in the waters and meconium from the baby's first bowel movement – a tell-tale sign that the baby was in some kind of distress. The blood ("port wine" as Dr. Sands quaintly put it), was a potentially serious sign of the placenta abrupting from the wall of the uterus. If this situation was left unaddressed, severe hemorrhaging might occur and the placenta could tear at the site of the umbilical cord. This, in turn, would adversely affect the baby's oxygen supply.

Suddenly things began to happen very fast. Dr. Sands was calm and firm. A cesarean would have to be performed immediately. This was urgent but not an emergency, as the baby was still doing fine. Throughout the day, the fetal heart rate monitor had indicated a steady and healthy beat. The room quickly filled with nurses as Naomi and Frank tried to process what was happening. They had only minutes to adjust to the reality that Naomi was about to have major abdominal surgery and give birth to her baby. The couple had absolutely no time to themselves as she was being prepped with surgical paraphernalia at lightning speed. Tears streaked her face as Frank and I reassured her again and again that she had done everything in her power to have a vaginal delivery. This was beyond her control.

Within ten minutes she was being rolled into the Operating Room. Frank was to wait outside while she got her spinal anesthetic. This would permit her to be awake for delivery and would allow Frank to be present also. The "spinal," however, did not take immediately, so for the safety of the baby, she was given a general anesthetic. Surgery would be performed *immediately*. This meant that Frank was obliged to wait outside during the entire procedure, which was agonizing for him.

Happily, at exactly 7:30 pm, Marcel was delivered – a beautiful, strong, healthy baby weighing 7 lbs 7ozs (Naomi's predicted weight for her baby) and measuring 21 inches long. His Apgar scores were 9 and 9, the highest a newborn can be given. Frank was able to hold his son immediately after he was taken out of the Operating Room. It must have been a bittersweet moment for him. He was holding his precious little son for the very first time, yet his partner was lying unconscious only a few feet away. Frank, speechless with admiration for his son, went to the nursery with Marcel to watch him being bathed and checked out. Meanwhile, Dr. Sands sutured Naomi and completed the surgery.

By 8:00 pm Naomi was in the Recovery Room, groggy and in a great deal of pain. She drifted in and out of coherence and sleep and was regularly checked by the pleasant Dr. Joshua Greystone, a resident OB. Frank dealt with the cord blood package and made regular visits to the nursery. I stayed with Naomi and had several rather peculiar conversations with her, as her confused thoughts wandered from here to there. She needed to rest, but her pain, coupled with the shock of what she had just endured, kept her befuddled mind too busy for real sleep.

At 9:30 pm Zaid administered a small dose of Phenergan, which relaxed Naomi enough to send her off into sweet sleep. By 10:00 pm, she was ready to be moved into her postpartum Room 148 and get settled for the night. She drifted in and out of deep sleep and occasionally awoke with a start, thoroughly dazed and confused by her surroundings.

At 11:00 pm, Frank proudly brought Marcel in to visit with his Mom. Naomi responded with a perfect smile as Frank handed her the baby. She was still very much under the influence of strong pain medication and our attempts to put Marcel to the breast were not very successful. Naomi needed to wait until she was more coordinated and less sleepy. Frank adapted to the situation and calmed his son down by walking around the room and talking to him sweetly. Marcel gazed up adoringly into his dad's sparkling but weary eyes. Clearly, the most important thing for everybody was to sleep. Marcel could wait a few more hours for his first feeding and no harm would be done. Frank took Marcel back to the nursery at 11:30 pm and I helped him get the room's pullout bed ready so that he, too, could get some much-needed sleep.

It was an amazing experience to spend this incredible day with Naomi and Frank. Their quiet determination to birth in their own natural way was matched by their courage and strength to adapt to unforeseen circumstances. Above all, they never lost sight of their ultimate goal – the joyful arrival of their beautiful, precious son. Naomi, you labored hard all day, never giving up, never allowing yourself to be overwhelmed. You both remained calm and strong during the labor and the birth. I thank you for allowing me to be part of this incredible and wondrous experience that brought so many challenges and joys.

"**Overwhelmed** and exhausted, Evan decided that the only way she could truly rest, would be to have an epidural."

JONNY'S BIRTH

As all moms know, Motherhood requires self sacrifice and "doing whatever it takes" for the sake of our offspring on a daily basis — at least until the kids are raised. This enormous commitment to our children begins with various discomforts of pregnancy and is in full swing by the time we experience our first labor pain. It is during the process of labor that so many women courageously display their selfless strength, as did Evan, who was willing "to do whatever it took," to bring Jonny into this world.

Shortly before midnight on September 21st, Evan's waters broke and she began to have mild, irregular contractions. In a phone call to her doctor, she was told that because her waters had broken, she should immediately go to the hospital. Real labor had not yet begun, but given the situation, Lars called me shortly before 1:00 am to let me know what was happening. I prepared my doula bag and wrote notes to my kids, fully expecting that I would be leaving at some point during the night.

After Evan checked into her room at the hospital, her contractions remained irregular yet persistent, thus preventing her from getting any real sleep. Lars was able to snatch a couple of hours, but they must have both felt tired when morning came around. I called at 7:30 am and Lars told me that a new nurse had just arrived and they were talking about induction to speed the labor up. I arrived at 8:15 am, at the same time as Dr. Kaur, who examined Evan and pronounced that the baby was still high up in the pelvis at -3 station. (The baby has to move down from -4 through 0 to +4 station). Her cervix was 50% effaced (with a goal of 100% necessary for dilation to be completed). Furthermore, she was 1½ cm dilated (with a goal of 10 cm for the baby to be delivered). Her cervix was still posterior and thick (it needed to be more anterior and thin). All in all, it was obvious that there was a long way to go before this baby was going to be born!

Because Evan's waters had broken, we had a timeline on our hands of about 24 hours. With this in mind, her doctor recommended that Evan would benefit from Pitocin induction. Pitocin is a widely used medication that induces contractions to dilate the cervix. At 8:30 am, a small amount of Pitocin was administered. Subsequently, a larger dose was given at 9:00 am, once it was established that Evan was having no adverse reaction.

Evan and Lars were being taken care of by Jessica, a student nurse under the supervision of Jung, the Labor and Delivery nurse. We were lucky to have Jessica, who was cheerful and personable – and because she was a student, had more time to stay with us to explain what was happening. Nine babies were born on the ward that day and it soon became clear that the nursing staff was overstretched and very busy. They rushed in and out of our room, somewhat distracted and often in a hurry. Jessica's continuous presence was reassuring and greatly appreciated.

At 10:00 am, the contractions were getting stronger and closer together and it seemed like labor was finally kicking in. Evan was focusing beautifully during each contraction. I rubbed her feet with ginger and mint foot lotion while Lars remained at her head, whispering words of encouragement and holding her hand for reassurance. By 11:00 am the contractions were three minutes apart and everything was going well. We were appointed a new nurse, Barbara, who wore a friendly smile and had a very upbeat manner. Aware of the importance of remaining mobile, Evan tried sitting on the birth ball – no easy feat while strapped to monitor belts. Unfortunately, she did not find this position very comfortable and returned to the bed, which she preferred.

At 1:00 pm, Dr. Kaur returned and examined Evan again. She was at 4 cm and the baby's head was lower. This was good progress but we still had a long way to go and Evan was exhausted from all her hard work and lack of sleep. Facing the reality of the situation, she decided to try a dose of Stadol, a narcotic that dulls the pain of contractions and makes sleep possible. Within seconds of the dose being administered through her IV, Evan fell asleep.

The Stadol, unfortunately, turned out to be a "double-edged sword." At first, it seemed to work wonders. She was restless during the contractions but remained asleep nonetheless. Then her skin began to itch – a common side effect of Stadol. Still asleep, she became extremely agitated during the contractions. Soon, she was whipping her sheets off and scratching her abdomen, as if she were having a wild dream. By 3:00 pm, she was beginning to wake up during contractions and clothing of any kind became unbearable for her. She even tried to rip off the abdomen band that was holding her monitor belts on. Barbara cut the band off with a pair of scissors and used two thin belts instead.

At 3:15 pm our student nurse Jessica was replaced by Kim, another new nurse. The Stadol was wearing off now and Evan's contractions were becoming very painful. Lars squeezed her hand hard as she moaned and worked beautifully through the overwhelming sensations. At 4:00 pm, Kim examined Evan again and pronounced her to be 4–5 cm dilated. This was normal, good progress, but still, it meant that we were not half way there yet.

Overwhelmed and exhausted, Evan decided that the only way she could truly rest, would be to have an epidural. Dr. Scott, the anesthesiologist, was summoned. I will never forget how he swept into the room, giving orders like an army General. Evan was in a lot of pain and it must have been very challenging to follow his complicated directions. But she did wonderfully and by 5:00 pm she was comfortable and sleeping. Dr. Kaur checked her and she was already 6 cm and 90% effaced and the baby was at -2 station. An hour later, she was 8 cm dilated and 100% effaced and the baby was at -1 station. This was fantastic progress and we all felt very encouraged. Evan was relaxed and resting and Lars was able to go and get some much needed nourishment in the hospital cafeteria.

Nurse Jung returned to take care of Evan. Lars kept getting her confused with Nurse Kim – we had seen so many nurses that day! The Pitocin was turned up again to keep the contractions coming fast and strong. Dr. Kaur came in at 6:45 pm and checked Evan. She was fully dilated with just a small lip of cervix left and her baby was down at 0 station. Evan decided to wait another thirty minutes before starting to push. She wanted to mentally prepare herself, gather up her strength and give the cervical lip a chance to move out of the way.

At precisely 7:20 pm, Evan began pushing her baby out. She was still completely numb from the large dose of epidural anesthetic that Dr. Scott had given her, so it was challenging to push effectively. Carefully following Dr. Kaur's instructions, however, she made a monumental effort with each contraction to bring her baby down. Lars and I each supported a leg and Lars counted to ten, three times with each contraction, to help Evan focus on her task. She had begun to develop a fever and it was now steadily rising. Fevers are not terribly uncommon in labor and this one was likely caused by one of two things: a side effect of the epidural medication; or the presence of infection.

Two hours had now passed, with Evan pushing hard through each contraction. The baby was doing fine, but he had not moved down the birth canal one iota. Dr. Kaur explained that Evan could continue pushing, but it was unlikely that the baby would move down any farther. Moreover, her rising fever was a concern and it was feared that it might become a problem. A better option, the doctor said, might be birth by cesarean. Evan and Lars spent some time weighing the situation and together they decided that under the circumstances, a cesarean delivery was the best choice.

Dr. Scott, the anesthesiologist, was called back and nurses rushed off to prepare the Operating Theatre. Evan and Lars, who were entirely caught off guard, had only a few minutes to adjust to the new situation. Despite this unexpected turn of events, their spirits never flagged and I could see that Lars was excited that he would soon see his son. My heart went out to Evan, who was completely exhausted after all her incredible pushing efforts. She was falling in and out of sleep between contractions, which she was once again beginning to feel. The epidural was starting to wear off, but it would only be a matter of minutes before Dr. Scott would be topping it up to surgical level.

At 10:00 pm, Evan was wheeled off to the Operating Theatre with Lars in tow, all dressed up in scrubs. I waited outside for less than half an hour and was rewarded by the most wonderful sight: Lars parading out of the Operating Theatre and beaming from ear to ear alongside his perfect, beautiful son! Lars followed Jonny into the nursery and I watched him warmly welcome his son. The new father crooned and talked to him, as he gently stroked Jonny's little limbs. Meanwhile, the nurse busied herself with all the various tasks that need to be done with a newborn.

Evan was wheeled out of the Operating Theatre at around 11:00 pm. She was very sleepy and her face glowed with satisfaction, despite her nausea and exhaustion. Jonny was finally brought in from the nursery and nursed with gusto for at least half an hour. I took some photos of the new family and left shortly after midnight, hoping that Evan would finally be able to get some real sleep. She had put in a tremendously long and hard day.

Evan and Lars, your adaptability and optimism never let you down as the day unfolded and new challenges loomed at every turn. Thank you for allowing me to be part of this amazing experience.

JACK'S BIRTH

"Patience is waiting. Not passively waiting. That is laziness. But to keep going when the going is hard and slow – that is patience." This saying comes to mind when I think of Jack's birth. In spite of discouraging setbacks throughout Lily's labor, she and her husband Brian courageously displayed a full measure of this precious virtue. I trust that their story will inspire you, as it has often inspired me, to keep going when the going is hard and slow.

The due day, January 11th, came and went with no signs of a baby wanting to be born. For some time now, Lily had been 75% effaced and about 1 cm dilated, but there had been no change over the past several days. (The cervix needs to efface from 0 to 100% and open from 0 to 10 cm to allow the baby passage through the birth canal.) She had tried everything in the book to encourage her baby to make a move after the 11th, from acupressure and nipple stimulation to massage and visualization. The only results were a few hours of irregular contractions followed by nothing. Lily's baby clearly needed a little more firm encouragement. Considering this obvious fact, she and her doctor decided that a week over due was long enough and an induction was scheduled for Friday, January 18th.

In preparation for the big event, Lily and Brian went into Healey Medical Center at around 7:00 pm on Thursday, January 17th to have a prostaglandin gel inserted. The gel softens the cervix and prepares the body for induction by Pitocin, a medication resembling the hormone oxytocin, which causes the uterus to contract. Upon their arrival, they were shuffled from one waiting room to another because the Labor and Delivery ward was overflowing and there was no space available for Lily. This must have been very frustrating and upsetting for them. After all, they could have stayed at home and relaxed until a room was available for them.

With their customary patience, they waited until Room 154 opened up for them at 9:00 pm. Finally, they were able to settle in. The gel was administered and by 11:00 pm they attempted to get some sleep. "Attempted" is the key word here, as it is not an easy option when monitor belts attached to your belly keep ringing an alarm whenever you move, and nursing staff are constantly coming in and out of your room. Needless to say, neither of them slept well for very long.

Lily was denied breakfast on Friday morning because labor was about to be induced and most obstetricians do not allow their laboring patients to eat. Pitocin was added to her IV line at 8:30 am by her nurse, Taylor. I arrived at 10:00 am and contractions were beginning to start up but seemed very manageable. The baby was still high up in the pelvis at -3 station (a baby has to move from -4 through 0 to +4 station in order to complete his journey to the outside world). We chatted and laughed and read our books, passing the time pleasantly enough. Lily even managed to talk through her contractions at this point and was in excellent spirits and excited about the day ahead. At 11:30 am, Brian went to get some lunch and took his time about it. It turned out his delay was due to the fact that he and another gentleman had gotten trapped in the elevator between two floors! Part of the rescue operation had involved climbing four feet up, out onto the upper floor. We joked about how it was a good thing there were no laboring women in the elevator, or that Lily had not been on the point of giving birth whilst her husband was trapped in a hospital elevator.

By 11:30 am the contractions were beginning to get a little stronger and Lily was teaching herself how to breathe nicely through them, focusing well during each contraction and still chatting happily between them. An hour later she decided that a position change would be helpful and moved to the chair. Positions were somewhat limited by the belts and paraphernalia, but Lily made the best of the situation. To her credit, she remained inventive at using all the possibilities available within a limited space. Dr. Gary Hanson came in at 1:30 pm to check Lily and we were all hoping that some progress had been made. Indeed, she was now 3 cm dilated, but the baby was still high at -3 station.

Dr. Hanson attempted to break the bag of waters which might have brought the baby's head down onto the cervix and caused stronger and more effective contractions, but owing to the posterior position of the cervix he was unable to perform this task successfully. He announced that he would come back in a couple of hours and try again. Lily must have been disappointed but she did not allow herself to become discouraged. She decided to try and take a nap while Brian and I continued to read our books.

Dr. Hanson returned at 4:00 pm to examine her again and said that there had been no change in two hours. This was *not* good news – especially in light of the fact that by now, Lily was receiving the maximum dose of Pitocin. This synthetic hormone *should* have been stimulating strong, effective contractions, but curiously, that was not the case. In fact, Dr. Hanson was so mystified that he used an ultrasound machine to confirm that the baby's head was indeed down in the pelvis. At this point Lily's determination and strong will really kicked in. She decided that standing upright was the most effective way of bringing her baby down, given that the doctor was still unable to break her waters. This position was also by far the most painful one to be in because it caused the contractions to be much stronger and to come closer together. Lily never wavered in her goal to bring that baby down. She stood up, leaned over a chair and swayed rhythmically as each contraction bore down on her. Brian and I stood by and watched, offering her all the love and support we could.

At 5:45 pm, a clot plopped onto the floor (perhaps it was the mucous plug dislodging) and from that point on, a steady trickle of fluid ran down Lily's legs. The waters had broken spontaneously! This was good news indeed and we hoped that the baby would move farther down into the pelvis, now that there was no fluid cushioning him in the uterus. As expected, the contractions became even stronger. Lily however, seemed more bothered by the unpleasant sensation of the waters leaking down her leg than by the intensity of the contractions — a strong woman indeed! She doggedly remained upright despite the pain and the steady trickle of fluid until Dr. Hanson returned at 6:30 pm. Surely, we all thought, progress should have been made by now.

Dr. Hanson examined Lily again and announced sadly, in a quiet and compassionate voice, that there was still no change. Lily had remained at 3 cm with her baby at -3 station, despite all her valiant efforts to make things happen. Dr. Hanson began to talk about the possibility of a cesarean delivery. He immediately sensed that Lily and Brian were not ready to give up yet and offered to leave it for another couple of hours. The baby was doing fine, so there was no urgency in the decision making process. Their "dream birth" was slipping away from them and it was challenging to readjust to new possibilities. I left them alone for a while to share their sorrow and frustration. When I returned fifteen minutes later, Lily was once again resolute in her willingness to keep trying, yet she was open to the possibility of opting for a cesarean. It took a lot of courage to accept this situation, and Brian helped her with his unfaltering and wholehearted support.

Again Lily took to her feet and leaned over the chair while Brian and I tried the double-hip squeeze to ease her pain and open her pelvis. I also tried some acupressure points on her shoulders to bring the baby down. Together, the three of us pulled every trick out of the bag, trying to make that baby move down. The new nurse, Mel, came on board at 7:30 pm and suggested side-lying, which sometimes helps to rotate a baby. Lily, who was exhausted from the intensity of contractions, readily agreed. Unfortunately, side-lying turned out to be even *more* painful for her. Sometimes, however, the most painful contractions turn out to be the most effective because they indicate big changes are occurring. Given that fact, Lily resolutely remained in the side-lying position despite the intense pain. Brian sat at her head and gave her all the love and support, while I sat behind her and put pressure on her lower back during contractions. At 8:00 pm Dr. Hanson came in again and checked her. We all waited with baited breath. *Surely,* these contractions with all their power and intensity *must* have made some major changes. In a sad, gentle voice, he quietly informed us that there had been *no change.*

Lily and Brian decided at this point that their baby was going to have to be born by cesarean and they adjusted to the idea quickly and gracefully. Dr. Runner, the anesthesiologist, came in at 8:15 pm to discuss the procedure with them. The couple then had a quarter of an hour to themselves, to prepare for the imminent birth of their son. Despite their disappointment, they remained cheerful and excited about the prospect of welcoming their baby within the hour.

At 8:45 pm, Lily walked into the Operating Room to be prepped with the anesthesia. Brian and I sat in the adjacent waiting area, on the edge of our seats – literally. Brian was dressed in his scrubs ready to join Lily at a moment's notice. I must say, he looked quite the part. At 8:55 pm Brian walked in to the Operating Room while I remained perched outside. Only fifteen minutes later, I spied him through the glass door as he strode proudly down the corridor behind his son, grinning from ear to ear and giving me two thumbs up. Off they went to the nursery and I continued to wait for Lily to be brought into the recovery room. Within minutes, news was spreading swiftly round the Labor and Delivery ward – 9lbs-14oz! What a big boy! Jack William had been born at 9:03 pm. He was 22 inches long, and yes, weighed only 2 ounces shy of 10 lbs! I saw Brian rush back into the Operating Room, obviously eager to tell the news of their son's weight to Mom!

Lily was finally brought into the recovery room at 9:30 pm and I kept her company while Brian was looking after Jack in the nursery. She was a little out of it to begin with, but soon became more coherent and told me about the birth – or at least what she remembered of it. She *did* remember Brian asking if it really was a boy! Finally Brian came in with Jack and at about 10:00 pm, mother and baby were reunited in a sweet moment and a gentle caress. Mel helped him to latch on and he fed a little although it was awkward with all the medical equipment in the way. Brian held Jack and soothed him with his cooing and rocking – a natural dad who had fallen head over heels in love with his son. By 11:30 pm Lily was nearly ready to go to the postpartum room and settle down for the night and I left the new family in peace.

Lily and Brian, it was inspiring to witness your mutual support of one another and your incredible patience, hard work and determination. Equally moving, was your willingness to be flexible and to experience fully, the joy of Jack's birth, even though it was not "the birth of your dreams" – and the going was hard and slow.

"Women feel so vulnerable when they are in labor and are easily upset by harsh words and an impatient manner."

ROSIE'S BIRTH

"Be patient." "Embrace change." "Have a positive attitude."
These tidy gems of advice — as well-intentioned as they might be — are much
easier said than done. We've all dispersed such seeds of wisdom, but it's less
than likely that they fell on fertile ground. Most people have difficulty seeing
past their immediate challenges in order to seek out a path of deliverance. A
rare few, however, manage to keep their end goal in view and muster the cour-
age to actually be patient, embrace change and have a positive attitude, in spite
of their pressing difficulties. Such was the case for Cheryl and Brandon, whose
birth plan flew out of the window point-by-point, until there was nothing left
except for the two most crucial elements: a healthy mom and a healthy baby.

The July 16th due date came and went; July 23rd came and went — 41 weeks and still no baby, not even a peep, no sign, no regular contractions, no show, nothing. Clearly the baby was perfectly happy where she was. An induction date was scheduled for 41 ½ weeks, which loomed on the horizon. In the hope of getting labor started, Cheryl tried everything from massage to acupressure and acupuncture — all to no avail. Induction day arrived and Brandon and Cheryl headed off to St. Paul's Hospital in New Calton at 6:00 pm on July 27. They arrived with a swarm of other couples that were either in labor or scheduled for an induction. Cheryl was not at the top of the list as she had "misunderstood" the 6:00 am appointment to read 6:00 pm. (Actually, her physician agreed that 6:00 pm was a much more sensible time to start an induction and she was told by the aforementioned physician to just turn up at 6:00 pm regardless of the scheduled 6:00 am instruction). There ensued a frustrating 4½-hour wait before Cheryl could even be admitted. Laboring women took prece-dence; scheduled inductions (at the "correct" time) took precedence, and Brandon and Cheryl watched as others who had arrived after them, were admitted before them. Finally, they were admitted to Room 1 at about 10:30 pm.

Cervidil, a prostaglandin suppository, is used to soften the cervix before a Pitocin induction. Pitocin is the synthetic form of Oxytocin, the hormone that causes uterine contractions to occur. So at 11:30 pm, Cheryl at last was given her Cervidil and had to lie still for two hours while the suppository absorbed — not a very comfortable position when you would love to get up and go to the bathroom. By 1:00 am, Cheryl was settled in for the night and Brandon left to go home and catch a few hours of much needed sleep. Cheryl had a fitful night of rest with constant interruptions from nurses, as is so often the case in a hospital setting. The Cervidil was to be left in place for 12 hours before Pitocin was to be administered, so Brandon and Cheryl spent a quiet morning together resting. Cheryl was not permitted to eat anything because of the impending administration of Pitocin. Suddenly, ice chips took on a whole new meaning because that was all she was allowed. Throughout the entire day, she enjoyed mountains of ice chips, lovingly fed to her by Brandon on a white plastic spoon. She talked longingly of snow cones, as if they were the ultimate in culinary perfection which I suppose they would be if ice chips were your limit.

At 11:00 am, Cheryl was able to get up and shower and prepare herself for the Pitocin. During this time, there was a lot of texting going on in with her work colleague Sian in engineers' lingo. We laughed over the engineering terminology that Brandon and Cheryl brought to the labor room and at the text messages going back and forth. The atmosphere was cheerful and upbeat.

At 12:30 pm, Marcia began the Pitocin, in the form of a continuous drip into the IV. Every 35 minutes she would return and up the dose by 6 ml. By 4:00 pm, we were at 30 ml and Cheryl was beginning to feel the contractions. She stood up and swayed from side to side next to the bed for each contraction — a beautiful dance to watch. Then, to everybody's shock and surprise, Cheryl stood up out of the rocking chair at 4:50 pm and her waters broke, producing the proverbial puddle on the floor. Cheryl was very distressed by the mess on the floor. A bossy unknown nurse waltzed in (we presume our nurse Marcia was busy elsewhere) and *ordered* Cheryl not to be embarrassed by the puddle. We nicknamed her "The Tornado." The nurse then proceeded to give Cheryl a completely inappropriate pep talk on the messier elements of labor, which did not help at all. Cheryl was very upset for a while by this unexpected turn of events. Brandon and I tried to acknowledge her feelings while at the same time encouraging her not to be so upset by the natural occurrence of the waters breaking. In fact it was a marvelous and positive sign that labor was really progressing and that now there was no turning back. Perhaps this was a frightening thought for Cheryl, as it might be for many first-time moms. Various nurses, including one named Phyllis, came and turned up the Pitocin every half an hour or so.

By 6:00 pm, Cheryl was working really hard with the contractions as they became more and more intense. She breathed beautifully and spent most of the time sitting in the rocking chair, rocking to the rhythm of her contraction, while Brandon sat op-

posite her on the bed, holding her hand and giving her constant words of encouragement. As with all women in labor, these words of encouragement sometimes helped
and sometimes irritated her. This kind of emotional flip-flopping is an excellent sign
that labor is progressing. With all this hard work, no food and little rest, Cheryl was
beginning to feel extremely tired.

Dr. Simpson came in at 6:45pm and checked Cheryl. She was almost 1 cm dilated
and the baby was still high at -3 station. The cervix has to dilate from 0 – 10 cms
and the baby has to move down from -4 though 0 to + 4 station in order to be
delivered. So Cheryl had a very, very long way to go and she felt extremely tired and
discouraged. So she decided to try a narcotic to help her relax and sleep a little. This
would take the edge off the intensity of the contractions and hopefully allow her to
recuperate a little. At 7:00 pm, Marcia administered the Stadol and then left us as her
shift had ended. She was replaced by Lorraine.

The Stadol did indeed help Cheryl to relax but only for a very limited period of
time. She slept for about 10 minutes but by 7:15 pm, she was stirring uncomfortably
during contractions and feeling disoriented and confused. She did, however, doze
between contractions and once she was corpus mentis again and the mental confu-
sion had subsided, she got into a great rhythm of breathing through contractions with
Brandon's help and resting quietly between them.

A very intense 2 hours ensued and I could sense that major changes were taking
place. Sure enough, Lorraine came in at 9:00 pm and examined her – and to our delight, Cheryl was 5cm dilated, 100% effaced and the baby had moved down a little to
-2 station. This was incredibly fast progress. No wonder Cheryl was feeling the contractions so intensely. She was becoming more and more exhausted with the level
of the contractions and only found a little comfort by lying on her side. I exerted
counter-pressure on her lower back and Brandon talked to her and tried to keep
her calm and focused. She kept saying over and over again "It hurts so bad. It hurts
so bad." Such rapid progress is overwhelming and Cheryl decided that she needed
to get an epidural in order to be able to have real pain relief and sleep.

Anesthesia was called and at 10:00 pm and Dr. Raven arrived to administer the
epidural while Brandon and I waited in the corridor, our ears straining to hear what
was going on in Room 1 with Cheryl. Finally at 10:30 pm, we were allowed back in
and found Cheryl looking much more comfortable although she was still feeling a

little pocket of pain on the right lower back and hip area. Her blood pressure had dropped radically, a common side effect of the epidural, so she was obliged to sit up in bed until 11:00 pm, which meant that she couldn't rest immediately. At 11:15 pm, a different anesthetist came and gave her a top up of epidural to quell the pocket of pain. At long last, she was able to lie down and rest properly.

Brandon settled himself on the uncomfortable window bench and I lay down on some cushions on the floor. Finally, all three of us, as if at a makeshift slumber party, were able to rest peacefully for a couple of hours. Lorraine came back in at 1:00 am to check Cheryl and announced that she was now between 7 and 8 cm dilated. Steady progress was being made and everything was on track. At 2:15 am, Lorraine checked her again and she was 8cm. The baby's heart rate was decelerating a little with contractions so Cheryl donned yet another piece of apparatus, the oxygen mask. An internal fetal monitor was put in place, which picks up contractions more accurately than the external monitors. We all went back to "sleep" for another couple of hours. By 4:00 am, Cheryl was beginning to develop a fever, a not uncommon side effect of having an epidural, or possibly a sign that she was developing an infection. An antibiotic was administered to add to the cocktail of medicines and paraphernalia to which Cheryl was now being subjected. She began to feel pain again – but this time there was a pocket on her left hip and low back so the anesthetist returned once more to give her another top up from which she obtained comfortable relief. Those anesthetists are really popular guys!

Dr. Simpson was supposed to be working till 8:00 am but there were so many women in labor that Dr. Guiterrez was called in early and marched in to check Cheryl at 6:00 am. To our dismay, Cheryl was still at 8cm and the cervix was thick and the baby still high at -2 station. This was not good news and Dr. Guiterrez did not mince her words. She was going to give Cheryl one more hour to progress and then if nothing had changed in an hour, we would be talking about cesareans. Dr. Guiterrez, while no doubt an excellent physician technically speaking, lacked compassion and patience and had the communication skills of an oaf. She made me think of an elephant in a china shop. Women feel so vulnerable when they are in labor and are easily upset by harsh words and an impatient manner. Cheryl was distraught at this abrupt and distressing turn of events. Anesthesia was called in once more for another increase in the epidural. The plan was to get her comfortable enough that Lorraine could turn up the Pitocin to a higher level and push for further dilation. By 6:30 am, she was comfortable again and on a high dose of Pitocin. We all did our best to rest once more.

At 7:15 am, Dr. Guiterrez stormed in again, checked Cheryl and announced that there had been no change. The baby's head was still high and "molding," which meant that for some reason, she was not coming down into the birth canal. So, she was going to perform a cesarean. Period! There was no gentle explanation, no time to adjust to the new situation, only a matter-of-fact "this is what we are going to do," as if having a cesarean was something one did every day. Cheryl and Brandon were very upset and I tried to reassure them that they had done everything possible to make this birth happen vaginally. Dr. Guiterrez came back in and gave her a "pep talk" on not feeling like a failure, which was to the point and brutally honest. Perhaps it helped Cheryl a little but I wished she could have just given her a hug and told her how sorry she was instead.

At 7:30 am, Lorraine left and our new nurse, Leigh came in to prep Cheryl for surgery and give Brandon his scrubs, which barely fit his tall frame. Brandon and I followed Cheryl's gurney down to the entrance of the OR, whereupon we were left to wait for five minutes while they continued to prep Cheryl in the OR. We had an interesting discussion on the challenges of parenting in those five minutes. Finally, the nurse came and fetched Brandon. I went out to wait for them in the corridor.

Brandon reappeared 20 minutes later, beaming from ear to ear, tears of joy in his eyes as he proudly wheeled his beautiful perfect daughter down to the nursery. Rosie Katherine had been born at 8:00 am precisely and weighed 7 lbs, 11 oz. She was 20 ½ inches long. The surgery had gone smoothly, and by 8:30 am Cheryl was in the Recovery Suite. Her vitals were monitored regularly and Brandon remained lovingly at her side. Dr. Simpson explained that Rosie had been presenting with a brow presentation, her head extended instead of flexed and this is why Cheryl had remained at 8cm without the baby being able to move down into the birth canal. A cesarean birth is frequently the only option in these circumstances. Cheryl had done everything humanly possible to birth her baby vaginally but Rosie was quite simply not in an optimum position.

After a couple of hours, Cheryl was wheeled into her postpartum room and finally at noon, she was able to hold and to fall in love with her wonderful daughter. Despite the tough 24 hours she had just been through, she was cheerful and upbeat and excited to have become a mom.

This was a roller coaster of a ride for Cheryl and Brandon with many bumps along the way. Nothing had gone as planned and yet they met every challenge head on. They always asked the right questions and remained in control of the decision making as much as possible. Both of them constantly looked out for one another and were an awesome team, filled with devotion and mutual support. It was such an honor to be able to work with both of you during this amazing, exciting and challenging adventure. I was so impressed by your ability to adapt to the new realities at each turn of events and your unwavering priority of always doing what was best for Rosie. Thank you so much for allowing me to be part of this very special day.

Twin
BIRTHS

"Despite being in the high-tech Operating Room, Farah found herself surrounded and protected by a group of women who trusted in her ability to bring her babies into the world."

ANWAR AND LIYANA'S BIRTH

For as long as mothers have been giving birth, their strength to do so has been bolstered by their own close-knit communities of personal support – family and friends, who love and sustain them through the rigors of labor. In our modern world of high-tech, brightly lit, clinical birthing environments, it is rare to see what I would call, a "traditional community" of birthing supporters. Most hospitals today restrict the number of people who can actually attend a birth. So it was truly a heartfelt privilege to be included as Farah brought Anwar and Liyana into this world. She did so in the same way mothers have given birth for countless millennia – with her own, very special community of love and support.

Farah's waters broke with a trickle early on Tuesday morning. At first, she wasn't sure that this was what had happened, but when she called the midwives, they told her to wait and watch for an hour and then call again. By the time the hour was up, it was fairly clear that there *was* a leak in the bag of waters. With that, the countdown clock began ticking, so the midwives, Patsy and Linda, told her to come in to Manchester County Hospital in Chesham where her babies were to be born.

I pulled into the parking lot at 9:00 am and whom should I see standing quietly on the sidewalk, but Farah, surrounded by her sister Yumna and her mom, Nadine, who had driven her to the hospital. She had just felt a huge gush of fluid, which confirmed that the waters had indeed broken. The four of us ambled up to the third floor maternity ward and settled in to Room 331. A young nurse by the name of Rose, greeted us and showed signs of disappointment that she was not going to be taking care of Farah for the day. The "top, senior" nurse, Sam, was going to be called in and Rose was merely in charge of the endless paperwork which has to be taken care of on admission. We all laughed hysterically when Rose asked, "Other than having twins, are you experiencing any major life changes at the moment?" Clearly, Farah was the "gem" on the ward that day, given that she was having twins and working with the homebirth midwives – everybody wanted to be involved!

Farah was put on the monitors and Patsy, the midwife on call for the day, arrived. Bindi, a student midwife, who was also going to be with us, accompanied her. We all chatted amiably for a while and there was a great feeling of excitement and anticipation in the room. Farah's contractions were coming about five minutes apart and she was handling them beautifully. Patsy and Bindi left us to go and get some breakfast and we settled in to a rhythm of chatting and quieting down for the contractions. I put some pressure on Farah's back as she leaned over the bed for each contraction and swayed to the tune of her labor. Nadine and Yumna sat patiently, figuring out the logistics of how the day was to unfold (as far as picking up big brother Zarar from school and other such details).

At 10:50 am Patsy and Bindi returned and it was time to check Farah. She had been 2 cm dilated for some time and was anxious to hear that progress had been made. (The cervix has to dilate from 0 to 10 cm, and thin out from 0 to 100% effacement and the babies have to move from -4 through 0 to +4 station.) It was extremely uncomfortable for Farah to be examined, but she did not complain. A huge grin spread across her face as Patsy announced that she was 5 cm dilated and the first baby was at -1 position. This was fantastic progress and she was already half way there and still smiling!

Rose came in and proceeded to insert a very painful Heplock into Farah's arm. A Heplock is an IV port, into which an IV line can be inserted. The reason behind this was to have a vein open in the event of an emergency. The procedure, unfortunately, was painful and her arm hurt persistently for the rest of the day. Feeling a little tired, Farah decided to try sitting in the rocking chair for a while. This was very comfortable and relaxing between contractions, but exacerbated her back pain during contractions, probably because of pressure from one of the babies.

Sam and her student nurse Sherri came in and introduced themselves. Farah, meanwhile, continued working hard with each contraction as they became more and more intense. She also managed to talk to various people on the phone and organize her son's day for him between contractions. She was also in regular contact with her husband, Tobias, who was stranded in London and unable to return to the USA until the following day. Obviously adept at multi-tasking, we could see that Farah was up to handling the task of raising twins along with Zarar.

At 11:30 am Patsy wheeled in the ultrasound machine because the Doctor had requested that she check the position of baby #2. He wanted to make sure that "he or she" was still head-down. A comical five minutes ensued as Patsy, a homebirth midwife, unversed in the technological side of modern obstetrics, could not figure out how to switch on the ultrasound machine. Having tried every knob and switch in sight, Sam the expert was called in and showed us a hidden button. She assured us that nobody ever could find it until shown. Sam had also been an ultrasound technician in the past, so she was quickly able to figure out that baby #2 was indeed still in the head-down position, and that both babies were neatly stacked in a perfect position for birth.

The next hour went by swiftly as contractions began to intensify and Farah's focus deepened. Nadine and Yumna decided to go to the cafeteria and get some lunch. Farah and I spent some quiet time alone. She tried several different ways of coping with the contractions, which she was feeling in her back. Standing up and leaning over the bed seemed to work well for her. I gave her counter-pressure on the areas of her back, wherever and whenever she needed it. The contractions were becoming more and more intense and her determination to work with the overwhelming sensations was awe-inspiring and beautiful.

At 1:00 in the afternoon, Patsy and Bindi returned with Linda, our other midwife, who was to stay with us and complete the team. Farah was beginning to feel some intense pressure with each contraction, so Patsy suggested another check. She was now 7 cm dilated, 90% effaced and baby #1 was presenting at -1 station! For the next ninety minutes we witnessed Farah's courage and incredible power as she labored through those last, tough, three centimeters. She moved around, rocked, moaned and cried — brilliant coping strategies for a woman in a non-medicated, intense labor. She never faltered in her quest to bring her babies into the world without drugs or interventions.

During each contraction, we would softly encourage her and tell her how incredible she was. Patsy had a gentle soothing mantra "*All is well Farah, all is well.*" Between contractions, we would sit in silent reverence. The atmosphere was one of joyful anticipation. Our homebirth midwives trusted absolutely in the innate wisdom of Farah's body to birth her babies. By 2:30 pm, Farah's urge to push was stronger, so Patsy checked her once more. Her cervix was very soft and she was 8 cm dilated. We all donned our shapeless blue hospital scrubs, ready to go to the Operating Room where Farah was to deliver her babies. The next half-hour was very, very tough, as Farah pushed through those last two centimeters. Nadine came to whisper words of encouragement, love and prayers to her between contractions. Likewise, the midwives and I would talk her through each contraction.

Finally, just before 3:00 pm, Farah decided that it was time to push these babies out. With her body primed for birth, we began the trek down the corridors to the Operating Room, pushing Farah in her bed. Yumna left to go and pick up big-brother-to-be Zarar and take care of him for the rest of the afternoon. We met up with the doctor in the corridor who was there in case of an emergency. He clearly understood that the midwives were to accompany Farah and he was only to intervene in the event of an emergency. He respectfully kept a very low profile. During our first five minutes in the OR, we experienced a flurry of rather stressful, intense activity. The anesthesiologist started hooking Farah up to various instruments at great speed as if there was already some kind of emergency. He was a little brusque and Linda tried to distract Farah from the high level of activity going on all around her. The priority was to keep Farah focused on pushing her babies out.

Soon, however, there was a cocoon of women around Farah, who was on the operating table. Patsy and Linda were supporting her cold feet, waiting patiently for the first baby. Bindi, Nadine and I were at her head, whispering words of encouragement and fanning her face with a packet of surgical gloves to keep her cool. The entire medical staff, except for one resident anesthesiologist who stood behind her, finished all their preparations for a possible cesarean and settled themselves in the doorway or outside in the corridor.

And so, despite being in the high-tech Operating Room, Farah found herself surrounded and protected by a group of women who trusted in her ability to bring her babies into the world. We were there to support her and encourage her as she toiled away at her monumental task. Little by little, Anwar's head came closer to the outside world, as Farah never wavered in her strength and determination. At 3:37 pm, Anwar slipped out and was placed briefly on Farah's belly before being taken over to the warmer to be checked by the pediatrician. Nadine followed him and watched as he took his first breath and cried out to us all, "I'm here!"

Farah's fierce contractions did not abate and she immediately started pushing again. The second baby's heartbeat dipped a little and Patsy requested that the anesthesiologist use some oxygen on Farah to help the baby. Within seconds, the heartbeat resumed its normal rhythm and all was well. Six minutes later, at 3:46 pm, Liyana appeared "sunny side up," which meant that she had been facing out frontward, inside her Mom. (This probably explains all the backache that Farah had been experiencing during her labor, as Liyana's back rubbed up against Farah's back *in utero*.) Liyana was taken over to the second warmer and checked by the pediatrician. Both babies were in perfect shape and scored 9 on the Apgar scale for newborns – the highest rating a newborn can score.

While the babies were being taken care of with Nadine watching over, Farah still had to push out her fabulously large placenta, which had nourished both babies for so long. It turned out to be almost as heavy as Liyana and it was no easy task for Farah, who, by now, was *exhausted*. After admiring the incredible placenta, Patsy then settled down to stitching Farah, which was an uncomfortable procedure. We tried to distract her with her beautiful babies, but she was apprehensive about holding them because she was shaking so hard from the monumental effort that her body had just exerted. So, we held a baby close to her face and helped her get through the painful stitching procedure as best we could.

Shortly after 4:00 pm, we formed a gorgeous procession through the halls of the Maternity Ward: Farah, with a baby under each arm; Patsy inexpertly steering them all back to Room 331; and Farah's entourage of female supporters. Finally, Farah was able to hold and feed her babies and fall in love with them all over again. Liyana was the first to suckle with great enthusiasm while her brother was being weighed and measured. He was a hefty 6 lbs, 5oz, 19½ inches long and his head circumference was 14½ inches. Next it was Anwar's turn to feed, but he was a little tired by now. He ate drowsily and with less gusto than his sister. Liyana, meanwhile, weighed in at 5 lbs, 5oz, was 19¼ inches long and her head circumference was 12¼ inches. Both babies were in perfect health and there was nothing left to do but hold them, admire them and love them. One of the nurses showed Farah how to feed them both using the football hold – one baby tucked under each arm. Nestled into their mother, they nursed happily for a while before being put into their cribs for a long nap.

At 6:30 pm, Zarar arrived with Yumna and Tobias' brother. Zarar was very excited and thrilled to meet his new baby brother and sister, and of course, was delighted to see his mom again. Soon we were moved across to the postpartum room and

Yumna took Zarar home to get a good night's sleep. The babies were sleeping, Farah at long last, was brought something to eat and everything was quiet and peaceful.

It was so beautiful to watch Farah giving birth to her babies with the strong and gentle support of her family. She trusted in the innate wisdom of her body to perform this incredible task and never faltered, even when the labor was at its most challenging. I am so grateful that I was able to travel on this amazing journey with you all. Thank you for allowing me the honor of accompanying you on this miraculous day. I wish you much happiness for your lovely family, *Inshallah!*

Sibling BIRTHS

"Chloe was an amazing support –

truly a natural doula in the way she acknowledged

her mom's feelings, while giving her

unerring physical and emotional support."

MARCO'S BIRTH

As "life events" go, few rival childbirth when it comes to establishing and strengthening heartfelt bonds. Natural bonding often occurs almost instantly between parents and their newborn. Likewise, new mothers and fathers are drawn closer to one another, as together they experience the birth of their child. Less common, but no less beautiful, is the special bond that can be formed between other family members – as was the case for this new mother and her teenage daughter.

Jasmin's waters broke at 4:15 am after several weeks of preterm labor, which had been more-or-less kept at bay by various medications. Jasmin had stopped taking any medications the previous Thursday, because they were no longer effective. She had been waiting patiently for true labor to begin, while all the time experiencing regular contractions twenty-four hours a day. Relieved that today would be "the day," she showered and dressed, and the whole family left for Launceston Medical Center, arriving at about 5:30 am. Johanna, the midwife on call for the day, examined Jasmin and pronounced her to be 4 cm dilated and 80% effaced. The cervix has to reach 10 cm of dilation and be 100% effaced to allow for the passage of the baby. So Jasmin was already nearly halfway towards the birth of her third child. The atmosphere was charged with excitement and bets were taken as to the time of birth. Chloe, the teenage big sister, chose 10:30 am. Jasmin herself, predicted 11:00 am. Chloe's younger brother Drew felt that his mother's choice was a bit premature. He added a whole minute to his guess of 11:01 am. Last, but not least, husband/father Tim, somewhat more pessimistically went for 3:45 pm.

I arrived at 6:00 am and found everybody calm and comfortable in a nice, spacious room, number 431. There they were at this early hour, watching basketball and chatting away with enthusiasm. Jasmin's contractions were beginning to get more intense and she was focusing really well by listening to her hypnobirthing music, which soothed and relaxed her. At 6:30 am Lisa, our nurse, took off the monitor belts and Jasmin was able to get up and walk around. Chloe and I took her for a circular stroll along the corridors and we peeked into the nursery and admired the babies. We walked round for twenty minutes and then returned to our room where Jasmin got herself comfortable on the physio ball, leaning over the bed. She listened to some beautiful soothing music that was positively soporific. The guys went off to get some breakfast and we settled down to a peaceful half-hour. Chloe dozed in the armchair and Jasmin worked calmly with her contractions as the waves of music flowed over her and relaxed her mind and body. Things appeared to be moving along at a steady pace and it seemed like there could be several hours of labor to go. With that, Tim and Drew decided to leave for a while and drop in at the office and at home.

Eight o'clock in the morning found us walking the corridors again with the contractions becoming more intense. Jasmin had to stop and breathe steadily every three or four minutes. By 8:15 am, she decided she wanted to return to the privacy of her room and sat on the birthing ball again. Chloe stayed close beside her, offering gentle words of support and encouragement to her mom. It was so beautiful to watch mother and daughter work in harmony and mutual respect in this way. By now we had a new nurse, another Johanna, who was to stay with us for the rest of the day. Johanna the *midwife* came in and examined Jasmin again and announced that she was now 5 cm and 90% effaced. This was steady progress but not a dramatic change. Little did we know what was round the corner!

It was time for Jasmin to go back on the monitors again. To everyone's delight, the baby's heartbeat was perfect, with just the right reaction to every contraction. In the uterus, a baby's heartbeat changes rhythm during a contraction and then settles back down to its normal pace as the contraction subsides. Suddenly contractions began to intensify and Jasmin requested some help in the form of counter-pressure in her lower back. Chloe sat on a stool behind her and pressed hard on her mom's back in exactly the right place during each contraction.

For the next two hours, Jasmin's contractions came fast and furious and Chloe stayed by her Mom doing everything possible to ease her discomfort. We used a heated belt on her lower back and took turns to apply counter-pressure. All the while, we offered her constant words of encouragement and praise. Chloe was an amazing support − truly a natural doula in the way she acknowledged her mom's feelings, while giving her unerring physical and emotional support. It seemed to me that things were moving really fast now. I quietly signaled to Chloe that she might want to go and phone her Dad and tell him to get back to the hospital pronto!

At 10:30 am, Johanna came back in and examined Jasmin once more. This time she announced that Jasmine was 10 cm and ready to push whenever she wanted! By now, Jasmin was on all fours. She was leaning against the top of the bed and began to make those tell-tale moaning and pushing sounds with each contraction. Drew and Tim had returned, and anxiously hovered in and out of the room. Chloe steadfastly remained at her mom's side, despite the rather alarming sounds she was making!

Within minutes, the urge to push became overwhelming and Jasmin moved into a semi-reclining position where she could pull her legs up towards her head, thereby helping the pelvis to open and allow the baby a safe passage through the birth canal. Chloe supported one leg and I the other, and with the help of both Johanna's, Jasmin focused on bringing her baby down and out into the world. She worked so hard and efficiently that the head was crowning by 10:45 am! The awed look on Chloe's face, as she saw the top of her brother's head appear, was priceless. We were all humbled by Jasmin's sheer power and strength as she brought her baby towards the light, centimeter by painful centimeter.

As the head slowly appeared, Johanna noticed that the cord was wrapped tightly around the baby's neck. With a quick, graceful motion, she clamped it and cut it before the next contraction. Then, with one more surge, Marco slipped out at 10:55 am – a perfectly beautiful baby with initial Apgars of 8 and 9 (an excellent score for a new-born). Drew and Tim rushed in and greeted him as he was taken over to the warmer to be checked. With tears of joy and relief, Chloe hugged her mom and congratulated her on the incredible feat she had accomplished. Tim cut the cord at its proper place and then we were expecting Marco to be brought over to Jasmin. To our dismay how-ever, the neonatal physician said that he wanted to take Marco directly to the nursery to be checked more thoroughly.

Meanwhile, Johanna was delivering the placenta and getting Jasmin cleaned up. A short while later, a nurse came in to explain that Marco was having trouble breathing by himself. It was necessary that he be ventilated and he would need to have vari-ous tests and X-rays done. In the heartbreaking absence of the baby, the family sat waiting quietly. It was a difficult time and yet everybody remained cautiously cheer-ful, anxiously awaiting more news. Time seemed to slow down to a crawl. We sat in contemplative silence in an agony of uncertainty about Marco's condition. Eventually, it turned out that Marco would have to be transported by ambulance to St. Paul's Neonatal Intensive Care Unit (NICU) in Whotten. Drew and Tim would follow in their car while Chloe, ever the doula, insisted on staying by her mom's side.

Before his departure for St Paul's, Marco was brought in with all his paraphernalia, so that Jasmin could get a glimpse of her son before he was whisked away.. It was heartbreaking to witness this and to realize that Marco could not lie in his mother's arms as Jasmin would have liked. His safety and well being, however, were of the utmost importance.

Shortly after Marco, his dad and big brother left for the NICU, we all settled down for some quiet time. I so admired the way in which Jasmin and Chloe managed to remain cheerful, despite this unexpected and difficult turn of events. Jasmin's mother-in-law soon joined us. At that point, I knew it was time for me to leave this family in each other's loving hands, to support one another. I am happy to say, that as it turned out, Marco soon thrived at the NICU and was able to be taken off all the machines. Before long, he was home with his wonderful family.

I would like to thank you all for allowing me to be part of this amazing journey. From this experience, there will be a very special bond between mother and daughter. Jasmine, what a marvelous lesson you have been able to give to Chloe for her *own* future journey to motherhood. Chloe, this poem is for you.

What is Support?
Support is unconditional.
It is listening…….
not judging, not telling your own story.
Support is not offering advice…….
It is offering a handkerchief, a touch, a hug… caring.
We are here to help women discover what they are feeling……
not to make the feelings go away.
We are here to help a woman identify her options…….
not to tell her which options to choose.
We are here to discuss steps with a woman……
not to take the steps for her.
We are here to help a woman discover her own strength……
not to rescue her and leave her still vulnerable.
We are here to help a woman discover she can help herself……
not to take that responsibility for her.
We are here to help a woman learn to choose……
not to make it unnecessary for her to make difficult choices. —Anonymous.

"Tears of joy rolled down Chloe's cheeks as she watched her **baby sister** appear.**"**

BELLA'S BIRTH

With the passage of time, I've become increasingly aware of the fact that the only thing in life that never changes...is the certainty of change. Whether we realize it or not, everything around us, every person we know, every experience we repeat, changes in some way from day to day. This truth is perhaps best born out (no pun intended) within the scope of my work as a doula. Every birthing experience is without question, unique unto itself. It can never be assumed that a woman will bear one child and the next, in exactly the same way – as was evidenced in the birth of Bella.

Like a bolt out of the blue, in the early afternoon of Thursday, December 18th, Jasmin experienced a huge contraction and went to her doctor to find out what was going on. Upon examination, she was 1 cm dilated and 70% effaced and Dr. Smith suggested she get herself to the hospital for a couple of hours to monitor the baby. Jasmine was given a large amount of fluid through an IV drip because early labor is often triggered by dehydration and will stop once the mother has rehydrated. Her contractions did not abate, however, and two hours later she was 2 cm dilated. It appeared that she was indeed in early labor, so it was decided that Jasmin should be admitted to Labor and Delivery. She was one day shy of thirty six weeks, which was considered a safe time for the baby to be born – especially in a facility like Middlefield Memorial Hospital, which boasts a state of the art Neonatal Intensive Care Unit, or NICU.

Jasmin's nurse was Beth, who was wonderfully supportive and quickly got permission for three of us to be present at the birth, when normally only two support people are allowed to be present. This meant that Chloe, Jasmin's eighteen-year old daughter, and I could stay with her throughout the entire labor. I arrived in the wind and rain at 7:00 pm and found Beth and Jasmin in Room 5 looking cheerful and excited. Jasmin was having contractions about every three to five minutes and they were uncomfortable but manageable.

Chloe and her dad Tim arrived at 7:30 pm. Chloe had just had her last class at 4:30 pm before winter break at college – what perfect timing! Beth attached a telemetry unit to Jasmin for monitoring purposes. This wireless device allowed Jasmin to be mobile, while being monitored continuously. Actually, the unit didn't have quite the expected signal range, and every time we wandered too far, Beth would come running to find us and bring us back within range. We did, however, manage to make a couple of trips to the nursery to gaze at two beautiful newborns in their cribs. Chloe and her mom caught up on all their news and Tim snoozed in Room 5.

At 9:00 pm, Jasmin decided to try and take a nap while contractions were still manageable. She put her headphones on and listened to relaxation music on her iPod. Meanwhile, Chloe and I watched *E! News* on TV and became experts on the top celebrity scandals of the year. By 9:30 pm the contractions were becoming more intense but farther apart – perhaps because Jasmin was lying down and not moving.

At 10:00 pm Chloe's brother Drew arrived and we continued to watch TV and chat for an hour. Since, it was clear by now that the baby was not going to arrive before midnight, Tim took Drew off to sleep at a friend's house nearby and the three of us settled down to try and get some sleep. A cot was brought in for Chloe who was able to fall to sleep quickly, while Jasmin and I dozed fitfully. Jasmin's contractions were too intense to sleep through. Moreover, we had constant visits from Beth who had to perform regular checks on Jasmin's vital signs. To make things worse, Jasmin was also suffering a severe throbbing headache, probably due to all the extra fluid she was being given in the IV and to the fact that she hadn't eaten for twelve hours. Her body was getting swollen from this excess fluid, especially her hands and feet. She asked Beth to get an order for Tylenol more than once but in the hustle and bustle of the evening, Beth kept forgetting to ask Dr. Smith.

Finally at 4:00 am, an order came through from the doctor to examine Jasmin and see what progress had been made. Judging by the intensity of the contractions and her three previous births, Jasmin should have been well on the way by this time. It was extremely disappointing therefore, when Beth checked Jasmin and announced that she was only 2 to 3 cm dilated and the baby was still very high in the pelvis. Dr. Smith recommended a small dose of Pitocin to induce a more active labor pattern. This was not a situation Jasmin had expected to encounter. Using Pitocin can lead to overwhelmingly strong and intense contractions. To make matters more difficult, Beth explained that the anesthesia team was on their way to a cesarean birth in the Operating Room. Jasmin had to decide *there and then* whether or not she might want an epidural because the anesthesia team would be completely unavailable for almost two hours.

Given that the Pitocin was going to be administered in very small increments, Jasmin decided to hold off on deciding about an epidural. Beth also let her know that should contractions become unexpectedly intolerable, she would hold off giving her any additional Pitocin until the anesthesia team was available again. Feeling somewhat reassured, Jasmin was given her first small dose of Pitocin in the IV and we waited to see what would happen. Chloe, having miraculously slept through all the comings and goings – and despite the room's cool temperature – awoke at 5:15 am. The Pitocin caused Jasmin's contractions to come closer together – similar to how they had been the previous afternoon. At 6:15 am, Jasmin got up to brush her teeth and freshen up. A new day of labor had begun. At 7:00 am, Dr. Knight, our new doctor arrived. An hour later, Cara, our new nurse, replaced Beth who was very disappointed to be missing the arrival of Jasmin's baby.

Jasmin's contractions continued to occur at regular intervals and the Pitocin was increased every half an hour or so in small increments. She was managing them beautifully with plenty of help and encouragement from Chloe and Tim, who himself had returned to us after snatching a few hours sleep at home. Upon her arrival at eight o'clock, Cara told us that Dr. Knight was currently performing surgery, but that she would soon be coming in to break Jasmin's waters. This was to be done in order to speed the labor. All these interventions were a far cry from the straightforward, fast labor that Jasmin had been expecting, but she accepted the unusual turn of events, composed and in good humor.

At 8:30 am, Cara suggested that Jasmin take a shower to relax and further freshen up. Half an hour later Dr. Knight arrived to check Jasmin and break her waters. To our dismay and bewilderment Jasmin was still at 3 cm, despite having had strong contractions all night long. Something was amiss. Jasmin was upset by the messy effect of her waters having been artificially broken and, compounded with her lack of progress in labor, she was becoming despondent. Moreover, her contractions started to come fast and furious after the waters were broken and they were proving very hard to deal with.

I suppose it was due to a combination of all these unexpected setbacks and frustrations, but at this point, Jasmin also became very fearful of birthing her daughter. She was assailed by flashbacks of the incredibly difficult time she had experienced during the first week of Marco's life at St Paul's NICU. She began to express all this angst and I gave her a stern "pep talk." "This was not last time!" "This was an entirely separate birth of an *entirely different* child!" "There was *absolutely no reason* to believe that the same problems would occur again!" Chloe was deeply moved by her mom's out-burst of profound anxiety. Both she and Tim hugged Jasmine and reassured her, while Nurse Cara and I encouraged her to release her fears, in order to allow this birth to move forward. After fifteen challenging and intense minutes, fraught with many tears, Jasmin bravely put her fears behind her and got back into the rhythm of her labor.

Contractions came on very strong and Jasmin took to deep breathing while I gave her counter-pressure on her lower back. She moved from bed to birthing ball and sometimes stood up and swayed. Eventually things seemed to be truly moving along fast. By this time, however, poor Jasmin was exhausted and weak from hunger and a constantly throbbing headache. She began to think that an epidural might give her the best opportunity for a much-needed rest. Cara came in to check her once more before Jasmin decided about an epidural. *If* she were close to the end, she would "soldier on" and keep going without it. Alas, she was only at a disappointing 4 cm. Such slow progress in so many hard hours! Without further hesitation, Jasmin opted for an epidural so she would be able to sleep and muster her strength for the birth. The charming and courteous anesthesiologist, Dr. Kamden, came almost immediately and gave Jasmin the epidural, which began to work very quickly. Ten minutes later, Tim and Chloe returned to the room to find Jasmin beaming from ear to ear and looking relaxed and happy. What a pleasant relief for us all – but especially for Jasmin!

Now that she was no longer feeling the contractions, Cara gave her a higher dose of Pitocin and we attentively watched the monitors. To our delight, they indicated that Jasmin was having incredibly strong contractions every two minutes and the baby was still tolerating the labor well. Indeed, the baby showed remarkable stamina and strength during the entire labor, despite all the medical interventions. Two pleas-ant hours passed, with time to talk over how *unexpectedly* things were panning out. Drew was with us once more and the family chatted happily together about this and that. With everything on an even keel, Tim took Drew off to get his flu shot in preparation for an upcoming mission trip.

At 1:30 in the afternoon, Dr. Knight returned and examined Jasmin once more. *This* time, the news was fabulous – Jasmin was at 8 cm, almost fully dilated and the baby had moved down to -1 station. (The baby moves from -4 to 0 then to +4 station in order to come out into the world). Within minutes of receiving this most welcome news, Jasmin began to feel pressure building up with each contraction. She was still experiencing no pain because of the epidural, but she could definitely feel intense pressure, which indicated that the baby was finally moving down the birth canal at top speed! Sure enough, at 1:45 pm, Dr. Knight announced that she could start pushing. This was somewhat perplexing to Jasmin, given the fact that she still had little sensation in her lower body. Her experience and her instincts took over, however, and push she did – with such force that we spotted the top of the baby's head on her first try!

Chloe held one of Jasmin's legs while I held the other and to our utter amazement, Bella's head appeared two pushes later. Tears of joy rolled down Chloe's cheeks as she watched her baby sister appear at 1:57 pm. Bella slipped out gently and gracefully and because of her premature delivery, the NICU doctor immediately checked her out. She was quickly proclaimed to be in perfect shape, with high Apgar scores of eight and nine. Two minutes later, Tim and Drew walked in to greet Bella. Moments later, they proudly followed her to the nursery where her blood sugar levels could be checked. A triumphant Jasmin pushed out her placenta and waited patiently while Dr. Knight performed a small repair. It was a time of relief and joy for everyone involved.

Within half an hour, a jubilant Tim wheeled Bella into the room, announcing that she weighed exactly 6 lbs and was 19 inches long. As soon as he handed her to Jasmin, she latched on to the breast like a pro. She proceeded to feed for more than an hour with such strength and determination, that we could already tell what kind of a woman she was going to be!

Jasmin, those twenty-four hours were an incredible journey for your whole family. So many unexpected turns in the normal course of labor! So *unlike* the three previous births! Yet, I witnessed a beautiful demonstration of your wonderful family's solidarity, support and love for one another, which enabled you to meet every challenge and relish the experience of ushering a precious new child into your loving arms.

"Dianne listened intently to the signals in her body, and moved beautifully to the sensations that were pouring over her, instinctively rocking her pelvis to encourage her baby to move down."

CHARLES' BIRTH

One beautiful aspect of life that I often have the privilege to witness, is the depth of love and connection that exists between a woman and man, in the hours surrounding the birth of their child. Dianne and her husband Joshua bring such beauty to mind and the memory of their palpable connection is one I will not soon forget.

Dianne started having some mild, irregular contractions at about 2:30 am on the morning of Thursday, June 8th. At first, her labor was quite forgiving and she was able to nap for a few hours between contractions. By 7:45 am, however, the sensations were coming more regularly and sleep was no more than a vague, elusive goal. At 11:00 am, the contractions were about five minutes apart but only lasting 30 to 40 seconds. (Good, strong contractions need to be three to five minutes apart and lasting at least sixty seconds for labor to be truly established.) Dianne was dealing well with them, breathing through them, and sometimes counting outloud as a distraction technique.

Checking in on her, I called at 2:00 pm and learned that the contractions were three to five minutes apart, but still not lasting the full minute. I arrived at Dianne's at 3:00 pm to find her being successfully distracted, not only by husband Joshua, but also by Joshua's brother Chris and his fiancée Theresa. The visitors soon left and Dianne started to become more focused on the early stages of her labor. She constantly walked around the apartment, carefully timing each contraction in a little notebook. She'd been doing this for several hours and it was clearly getting a bit tedious. I suggested that she'd know well enough when the contractions were lasting longer and she might want to take a break from record keeping.

Within an hour the contractions were becoming more intense and Dianne took to kneeling over her birth ball with an icepack on her neck to cool her down. Conversation began to dwindle, a sure sign that labor was truly setting in. Joshua took off to the shops for some last minute errands and Dianne tried lying on the sofa on her side, as she was already feeling the effects of a short night's sleep. She began to focus seriously on her contractions now, rubbing her hips and her belly as the powerful sensations swept over her. To her benefit, Dianne is also a massage therapist and a doula. Her expertise and knowledge came in handy as she gently stroked her belly and soothed the intensity of the contractions.

Half an hour later Joshua returned and Dianne felt it was time to start thinking about going to the hospital. Contractions were now regularly three to five minutes apart and lasting a full minute. So at 4:45 pm we helped Dianne into the front passenger seat of their car and she embarked on what was probably one of the most uncomfortable car rides of her life. Having contractions while seated in a car in heavy traffic is no picnic.

We arrived at Hosley Medical Center at 5:15 pm and were admitted to Room 418 by Nurse Jill who set Dianne up on the monitors and settled her in. Dr. Farley looked in at 5:30 pm and checked Dianne. She was 3 to 4 cm dilated, 100% effaced and the baby was at 0 station. (The cervix has to efface from 0 – 100%, dilate from 0 – 10 cm, and the baby has to move down from -4 though 0 to +4 station). At her last check, Dianne had been 2 cm dilated and 60% effaced, so she had made some progress during her day of early labor at home. Nurse Stella came in and introduced herself as our nurse until the next shift change. She then began the tedious task of asking Dianne and Joshua a host of questions about their health history, which they patiently answered between contractions.

Standing up was definitely Dianne's preferred position throughout the entire labor. She was obliged, however, to remain in bed during the period when the monitor belts were in place, to measure the baby's heartbeat and Mom's contractions. Fortunately, nurse Stella was open to Dianne getting onto her knees on the bed and there she stayed for at least twenty minutes. At 6:30 pm she was able to get off the monitor belts and immediately stood up. Every time a wave of intensity rushed through her, she would grab Joshua by the shoulders for support and sway rhythmically from side to side. She listened intently to the signals in her body and moved beautifully to the sensations that were pouring over her, instinctively rocking her pelvis to encourage her baby to move down.

It was awesome for me to be able to watch her sway and moan, a look of utter concentration on her face as she clung to Joshua who held her lovingly, a steady, grounded pillar of support. For the next two hours, Dianne and Joshua worked together in this way. With each contraction, Dianne gave Joshua an almost imperceptible beckoning with her fingers and he would swiftly rise up from his chair to stand firm for her. From time to time, I offered soothing words of encouragement to maintain the spirit of calm and quiet that hovered in the room.

At 8:00 pm our new nurse Beatrice came on shift. She was to remain with us for the rest of the night. As contractions became more intense Dianne decided that a warm shower might help. Indeed, she loved the sensation of the hot water pouring down her back and over her belly. She might have stayed there longer, but having been seduced by the delights of warm water, she opted for the Jacuzzi as a next step. To my amazement, Dianne's sense of humor never left her. I was particularly amused when she emphatically announced, "Being a doula is much easier than having a baby. I prefer being a doula!" For a while, she also had a fixation on the baby being born at 9:30 pm, but alas, this was not to be. In response to the Jacuzzi request, Beatrice announced that she needed to check Dianne first. If her dilation was beyond 7 cm she would not be able to go into the Jacuzzi, as it would be too close to delivery. We waited with baited breath as Beatrice checked her. She was 4 to 5 cm. dilated. So, the good news was that she could use the Jacuzzi. The bad news was that she still had a way to go before reaching full dilation.

At 9:00 pm Dianne entered the Jacuzzi tub and tried to find a comfortable position. Since lying on her back was her least favorite position, she tried going onto all fours in the tub, while Joshua used a large blue plastic bowl to pour warm water over her back. As it turned out, this was one of those ideas that "looked good on paper," but in practice was not terribly successful. Any wet, exposed parts of her body soon became chilled and staying on all fours in the tub was tough on the hands and knees. Undaunted, Dianne decided to get out and walk around, which was just as well because Dr. Farley had returned and wanted to check her. Being checked was always a trial for Dianne because it involved her lying flat on her back – the most painful position for her. True to form however, she assumed this position without complaint so Dr. Farley could see how far her dilation had progressed. As he did so, he broke her waters with an amniohook so that the baby's head would put more pressure on her cervix and hopefully speed up the dilation process. She was now 6 to 7 cm – steady, but fairly slow progress.

As soon as she was able to, Dianne opted to stand up and once again started her beautiful rhythmic rocking with Joshua as her support. Only now, the contractions were much more intense and coming much closer together, as the baby's head pressed directly onto the cervix with no soft bag of waters to cushion the pressure. Half an hour later, Beatrice checked her again, only to reveal yet another "good news – bad news" situation. Dilation had not changed, but the baby had moved down one whole centimeter to +1 station. This was good progress, but Dianne was beginning to feel discouraged that dilation was not happening more quickly. The intensity of the contractions combined with her lack of sleep and food were beginning to exhaust her. Beatrice suggested a shot of Stadol, a narcotic drug that would help her to relax and perhaps even rest a little. Stadol does not take the sensations away but it can soften their sharp edges. The effect it had on Dianne was not obvious to us, but as she explained later, she basically went off on a Stadol "trip" – visiting childhood experiences and memories, long buried in her subconscious. We were only aware of her eyes tight shut and lots of moaning and groaning during contractions. We had no idea of the cacophony of sounds and vivid images that she was hallucinating.

It must have been so hard for Joshua to watch the woman he loved experience such intense discomfort – even though it was "pain with a purpose." He never once allowed his support for Dianne to falter, although there were plenty of times when he no doubt would have preferred to have been "tripping" elsewhere himself!

At 11:00 pm the Stadol trip was beginning to wear off and Dianne's pain level was increasing rapidly. Beatrice checked her again and to our huge disappointment she was still at 7 cm. It was then that Dianne made the decision to allow herself a couple of hours of much needed sleep before the monumental task of pushing her baby out. The only way to obtain complete pain relief was with an epidural. With that, Will, the anesthesiologist, was called in and Joshua and I were asked to leave while Beatrice and Will administered the epidural.

We sat outside munching on a packet of potato skins and I realized just how difficult this was for Joshua to see Dianne working so hard and getting so exhausted. I tried to reassure him that everything so far had gone well – that progress had been slow but steady and that yes, labor is hard, hard work, but that Dianne was doing brilliantly. When we returned to Room 418 at midnight, Dianne was lying comfortably in bed. The epidural had worked its magic and Dianne was snoozing and barely noticing the contractions, which showed up on the monitor screen. Moreover, she was already at 8 cm! By 12:30 am Joshua settled on his pull-out bed. I was comfortable with pillows and blankets in the rocking chair and the three of us took a well-deserved nap. From time to time, Beatrice would creep in and do some paperwork or check on Dianne. At 1:00 am Dianne was feeling a lot of pressure and so Beatrice checked her – she was 9 cm dilated with a lip of cervix still in the way. Three quarters of an hour later,

Beatrice announced that Dianne was 10 cm dilated. Furthermore, the lip had gone and the baby had moved down even farther to +2 station. At long last, it was time to start pushing!

The first few pushes were not very effective as Dianne was totally numb from the epidural. In an effort to pick up the pace, Beatrice turned off the magic potion and within about half an hour Dianne began to get more sensation back. Now, more in touch with her body, she was able to start pushing in earnest. Joshua and I helped her by supporting a leg each, while Beatrice directed her pushing efforts to the right spots. Dianne was a quick learner and soon the baby was moving down the birth canal, slowly but surely.

Dr. Farley joined us at about 2:30 am and the time rolled on. Contractions came about every three to five minutes and Dianne would push with all the strength she had in her exhausted body, trying to relax and rest between times. To say the least, this is not an easy task, when such strange and intense sensations are occurring in your body as the baby moves down the birth canal. By 4:30 am we could see the top of the baby's head with lots of hair, but the entire head was not coming under the pubic bone. Meanwhile, Dianne was getting more and more exhausted with each contraction. Dr. Farley explained that the delivery needed to be assisted by a vacuum extractor, a suction device that pops onto the baby's head and helps to traction him out under the pubic arch. Dianne had been hoping for a normal vaginal delivery, but by now she so urgently wanted to get her baby out of the birth canal, she readily agreed to a delivery assisted by the vacuum extractor. The room was prepared for delivery as Dianne continued to push valiantly with all her might.

Finally at 4:51 am Charles was delivered onto Dianne's belly as Mom and Dad shed tears of joy and exhaustion. I cut the cord, which had been wrapped once round his neck. (Joshua's distaste for medical procedures afforded me this honor.) Charles was whisked over to the baby warmer to be checked out. He had fantastic Apgar scores of 9 and 9 – virtually the highest a newborn can get, which meant that he was in great shape. Joshua watched adoringly and took photos while the nurses weighed Charles and cleaned him up. He was 7 lbs 9.4 oz and a long 22 inches! I remained with Dianne while Dr. Farley delivered the placenta and stitched her up after a second-degree tear. At last, she was able to unwrap her newborn son and place his naked body next to her skin, where he nestled in to her and immediately enjoyed his first feeding with the gusto of a hungry, healthy infant.

It was an incredible experience to be able to work with the both of you. Dianne, you were so strong, never giving up even when the going got tough. Joshua, you were a steady loving support for Dianne. And, considering your aversion to blood and medical procedures, you were amazing the way you stayed there the whole time. You did everything Dianne asked and always appeared calm and steadfast, even though you probably didn't feel it! Thank you for allowing me the honor of accompanying you both on this incredible and wonderful journey. Thanks also for the special treat of being the one who cut the cord – a first for me!

THE SOMEWHAT RAPID
ARRIVAL OF EVANRAE BONT

I would be the first to admit that giving birth is no laughing matter. In practically the same breath, however, I would have to say that there are situations and personalities that can actually make labor and delivery quite funny – after the fact, at least. As revered as pregnancy and childbirth are, (and well they should be!) I've always felt it is healthy for us to be able to appreciate the lighter side of these experiences, when and if appropriate, of course. As a doula, I've experienced plenty of situations (even some of the more intense ones) that years later, can still raise a chuckle – or even better, a good, hard laugh. Among the more humorous anecdotes I might share with you over a cup of tea, would be the tale of Dianne and the somewhat rapid arrival of her daughter, EvanRae.

Dianne suspected that "things" were beginning to happen during the final days of the year and thoughtfully warned all those concerned that "it could be any time now." She could have never anticipated, however, that "when the time came," it would arrive with the *whoosh* of an express train.

For days, irregular contractions had been signaling her approach to the "final destination" of what had been a pleasant excursion through pregnancy. Not surprisingly, her visit to the doctor on December 29th had revealed that she was 1cm dilated and 75% effaced. This was a promising sign, but as the doctor pointed out, some women can be 1 or 2 cm dilated for two or three weeks before they have their babies, so it didn't necessarily mean that birth was imminent. Furthermore, the baby was still high in the pelvis at -2 station. With that, Dianne "settled in" for the remainder of her journey. (The cervix has to dilate from 0 to 10 cm, to thin out from 0 to 100% effacement and the baby has to move down from -4 through 0 to +4 station in order to come out into the world).

But only a few days later, on Friday, January 1st, Dianne began to have more regular contractions at 3:30 pm in the afternoon. She coped well with them and went about her business in the typical fashion of a second-time mom who understands that early labor can drag on for a very long time – and it's best to ignore it for as long as possible. So off she went with Joshua and son Charles to Rosamond's house for dinner, where they regaled themselves with a New Year's feast of Kielbasa, the traditional Polish sausage. In anticipation of a new year – and better yet, a new baby – spirits were festive. Dinner was absolutely delicious, but in retrospect, perhaps not the best choice for a woman in labor. As Dianne said, it was excellent the first time it went down!

By 8:30 pm the contractions were getting stronger and Dianne decided it was time to seek the solitude and quiet of her own home in order to focus on the task ahead. At home she took a shower that helped ease the sensations of the contractions, which were now coming every three to five minutes. Expecting a long night ahead, she tried to lie on the bed with little Charles and rest. But as is often the case, she quickly discovered that lying down is the most uncomfortable position imaginable for a woman in labor. Besides, Charles wasn't keen on the idea of sleep, being a little upset by his mom's unusual behavior as she breathed and focused through each contraction.

Dianne phoned me shortly after 10:00 pm, still very much in command of the situation but unable to talk during a contraction. This was a strong indicator that she was in active labor and I hastened to make my way over to her apartment. Meanwhile, Joshua drove to Dianne's sister Becky's house where Charles was to spend the night. Dianne was in no hurry to go to the hospital, but Dr. Farley had recommended that she come in because she was going to need prophylactic antibiotics as a result of testing Group B positive (GBS+), which indicates the presence of streptococcus bacteria in the birth canal. Twenty five percent of women test Group B positive when pregnant and 1% of their babies risk catching the infection during birth if not given prophylactic antibiotics.

When I arrived at about 10:15 pm I watched Dianne as she worked beautifully with her contractions. She would lean over the physio ball or the bed and breathe deeply, moaning a little and swaying her hips from side to side. Between contractions, she was able to talk and tell me about her strange day and even pass comment on *Prince Caspian* that was still playing on the TV in her bedroom. As attentive as ever to the needs of others, she offered me juice from the fridge and made a few amusing comments on the "return of the kielbasa." She was restless and I could tell that contractions were getting seriously hard to deal with as she moved from room to room trying to find a comfortable spot.

At about 11:00 pm, Joshua called and I heard him say on the phone that he was on the point of leaving Becky's, having settled Charles and fitted his toddler seat in Becky's car. My intuition kicked in and told me that we should not be waiting twenty minutes for Joshua to return to the apartment to pick us up. I quickly volunteered to take Dianne to the hospital myself and suggested that Joshua meet us there. Well into her labor, Dianne readily agreed to this plan, said goodbye to Joshua on the phone and we made our last minute preparations for departure to Hosley Medical Center.

I never realized how bumpy Amley Road was until I drove it that night with a laboring woman in the back of my car. I winced at each pothole in the road and tried desperately to avoid the major ones. Dianne sat in the back with her face in a pillow to muffle her groans as we sped and bounced along towards the hospital. I was so intent on avoiding bumps that I drove straight past it. In a fortunately timed moment while surfacing for air, Dianne noticed the hospital streaking by her window and had enough presence of mind to let me know. Needless to say, we lost no time in turning around.

I suggested we try parking and walking to the Emergency Entrance. Dianne did not need to be reminded of the importance of remaining mobile in labor and agreed to attempt the walk after I assured her we could stop for each contraction. It was quite comical to see her clutching a couple of road signs and leaning onto their yellow posts for the two contractions she had while walking from the car to the entrance. Even Dianne, in the throes of intense labor, saw the funny side and made a comment about the signs being thoughtfully placed for women in labor. Bless Dianne for never losing her sense of humor.

We arrived at the Emergency Room at 11:30 pm and Dianne made a bee-line for the bathroom while a nurse from Labor and Delivery was called to come and fetch us. At the same time Joshua arrived. Kelly the nurse, Joshua and I waited patiently outside the bathroom for Dianne to reappear. After a couple of minutes, we were beginning to feel concerned and I knocked on the door. Out came Dianne who had, understandably, been preoccupied with dealing with her contractions and was taking her own sweet time. She thrust her coat at me, grabbed her pillow back and announced she was ready to walk up to Labor and Delivery. No wheelchair for this awesome young woman.

The walk to Labor and Delivery was a trying one, with Dianne now having contractions every three minutes and needing to stop at regular intervals to breathe through the intensity of the sensations. Kelly wanted to get the monitor belts on Dianne and have her start filling out the numerous pieces of paper that accost the patient on arrival. This is no simple feat when your "patient" is in the throes of active labor. Kelly also needed to examine Dianne and see how far dilated she was, so that she could let Dr. Farley know what was going on. Dianne was incredibly good-natured about all this poking, prodding and questioning, despite being in intense pain. At 11:40 pm, Kelly announced to our great delight, that Dianne was now 7½ to 8 cm dilated. We could all see that labor was progressing at breakneck speed.

Dianne managed to get onto all fours on the bed, which was about as much movement as she could cope with given the restrictions of the monitor belts. Contractions were now relentlessly close together and Dianne, as if playing her labor in fast-forward, appeared to be passing through every stage of labor in a matter of minutes rather than hours. Joshua stood stalwartly at her head, cooling her with a washcloth and feeding her ice chips. I tried to encourage and reassure her during each contraction as the intense sensations completely overwhelmed her. At times she must have felt uncertain of her ability to get through it all, but I never doubted that she had the strength, stamina and courage to birth her daughter. Meanwhile, Kelly finished her shift at midnight and our new nurse, Linda appeared. We barely had time for introductions. Dianne's labor was now at full throttle.

About ten minutes after midnight Dianne groaned that she was feeling lots of pressure and an urge to push. Linda quickly phoned Dr. Farley to let him know. When Dianne had been checked at 11:40 pm, the baby was still high up in her pelvis. The fact that less than half an hour later she was feeling the urge to push, meant the baby was traveling well above the normal speed limit. This little girl was in a hurry and poor Dianne had to deal with those changes taking place inside her as the baby moved down through the pelvis at what must have felt like 90 mph!

Gone was the quiet focus of earlier contractions. Instead, her arms flailed around her head and she moaned and groaned as the surges overtook her entire body. Not surprisingly, there was a certain amount of screaming and yelling which the nurses ignored (I guess they get used to it) and which must have been upsetting for Joshua. I knew, however, that this was simply a sign that things were moving along excruciatingly fast for Dianne. Sure enough, when Dr Farley examined Dianne at about 12:25 am, he announced that the baby was at +4 station and he barely had time to gown up before we could see EvanRae's head appear. By this time Dianne was screaming, "just get her out" – a not uncommon expletive for a woman in this stage of labor. And out she came at 12:30 am exactly, a perfect baby girl with Apgars of 8 and 9.

Joshua cut the cord. It was a first for him because he had not wanted to do this for his son eighteen months previously. EvanRae was taken over to the warmer to be checked out. She weighed 6 lbs 15 oz and was 20¼ inches long. Her breathing was a little rapid, most likely a side effect of such a quick passage through the birth canal. Another possibility however, was that it could have indicated an infection, given the fact that Dianne's antibiotics had not had time to get into her bloodstream. With that, the pediatrician insisted that EvanRae be taken to the nursery for observation and Dianne was only able to hold her briefly beforehand. Within minutes of the birth, however, Dianne's humor was back on track. As Dr. Farley performed a minor repair with a few stitches, she gaily informed him that she hated him for what he was doing to her.

Once everything had quieted down we all felt shell shocked and stunned – especially because EvanRae was not in the room with us. We could barely grasp what had just happened. It seemed almost unreal that only an hour ago we had arrived at the hospital. And now, Dianne and Joshua were the proud parents of two children! EvanRae was finally returned to Dianne at 3:30 am, having been pronounced fit and well. Finally, after a fast-paced and exhausting trip to the outside world, she enjoyed her first feeding and settled down to snuggle with her mom.

Dianne, you were amazing. Your strength and courage were inspiring and I hope you are very proud of yourself. The power of a laboring woman never ceases to amaze me. Your good humor never wavered and your strength and fortitude were formidable. Precipitous labors such as this are extremely difficult to cope with and you worked so hard to allow your body to perform this monumental task so bravely. Thank you both for allowing me to be part of this incredible birth.

"The entire, perfect body of baby Rhiannon slipped out into the big wide world and into the capable hands of her Dad, who delivered her as if he had been doing it all his life."

RHIANNON'S BIRTH

They say "timing is everything" and nothing could be truer, especially when it comes to having babies. Throughout my years as a doula, I've witnessed both ends of the spectrum with regard to timing. Some babies have taken days to make their entrance. Others have suddenly "appeared out of nowhere"…or so it seemed. It all goes to show that labor is thoroughly unpredictable. The timing of a birth is, in most cases, up to the independent "will" of a woman's body and/or, that of the baby — and is usually beyond our control. Thankfully, for Fiona, the timing was favorable — albeit a bit hair-raising — for the sudden, speedy birth of Rhiannon.

In the still-dark morning hours of May 13th, in a remote, mountainous corner of the United States, Fiona's waters broke. Looking back, this could have easily happened in an even *more* remote spot, possibly in a tent or cabin far from anywhere. But she and Simon had decided to not stay for the "friends & family sleepover" which followed the Mother's Day hike and baby shower. Indeed, it was fortunate that they had only spent the day up in the nearby mountains and had decided to return home for the night.

Although unwilling to disturb the Birth Center at such an uncivilized hour, Simon and Fiona did finally phone at 4:00 am, and were told by the midwife Diane to head over. The moon was full and it must have been a spectacular drive from their secluded home in the woods, out to the highway. I wonder what must have been going through their minds during those hours. The birth of their baby would be imminent now that the waters had broken, and yet it was all so sudden — nothing was really quite ready and they hadn't yet agreed on a name (more on that later). Fiona was having mild and irregular contractions during this time and was dealing with them very well despite the rough, unpaved forest road.

Having been a few hour's drive from "civilization," they arrived in Westlake at around 7:00 am and went to their beautiful second home on Davis Avenue to wait for their call from the Birth Center. By now Beatrice was the midwife on duty and she told them to come in for a check-up. While at the Center, Fiona received only an external examination (the fewer internals the better, once the waters have broken) and then returned again at 10:15 am for her non-stress test to check that her baby was doing fine. This took some time as the baby insisted on sleeping throughout the whole procedure. Even a large dose of acidic juice only resulted in a few exclamatory kicks.

Simon and Fiona left the Birth Center at 1:30 pm, armed with a prescription for antibiotics. Because the waters had broken, Fiona would have to take the medication from 10:00 pm onwards if she had not yet gone into labor, to ward off any risk of infection. Clearly, this was not what Fiona wanted. In fact, for her, it was something to be avoided at all costs. They went off to the New Life Center to buy some snacks and then on to the pharmacy for the prescription. Quite suddenly, Fiona's contractions changed from being fairly easy to handle and at least five minutes apart, to becoming very much stronger and only a couple of minutes apart. I can only assume that it was the sight of that pharmacist preparing the aforementioned antibiotics that clinched it for her and pushed her into active labor right there and then!

With these powerful contractions coming on, they decided to skip the trip to the supermarket and go straight home, from where they phoned me almost immediately. I spoke briefly to Fiona and decided (wrongly as it turned out) that she was probably still in early labor. Because she was getting very tense and anxious, I suggested I might be able to help, by coming to spend some time with her, calming her down, getting her to rest a little. Perhaps then, I would return to her home later on in the afternoon after she had had a nap. As I got out of the car at around 1:20 pm, I heard a loud moaning and I thought, "Wow, this lady is going to need a lot of calming down!"

I had planned to put on some soft music, to suggest she lay down on the bed with her eyes closed, and offer some gentle massage and relaxation. This would give her a chance to recuperate and catch up on lost sleep and prepare for the many hours of labor that we were going to have to work through together. However, things did not quite turn out that way. I barely had time to shake hands with Simon before another overwhelmingly powerful contraction hit Fiona full on and she began making sounds that she had probably never made in her entire life. It was clear to me that things had started happening so quickly in her body, that her mind could not keep pace. She was having a really hard time.

We tried desperately to find a comfortable position for her, and eventually, leaning over the birth ball seemed to do the trick better than anything – although she was still having a really tough time with those contractions. There seemed to be no time to rest from one, before the next one would assail her full force and cause her to moan and groan in pain. She kept saying, "I can't do this," thinking, I suppose, that this was only the beginning. The unbeknownst truth of the matter was that she must have dilated to 10 cm during that single hour. No wonder those contractions must have seemed so challenging! I can only wonder at her strength and tenacity during that time.

Simon, in the meantime, was being wonderfully supportive. He was busy as a new-father-to-be, fetching everything we needed, holding her hand, squeezing her tightly to him and giving her endless words of encouragement. He is clearly someone who always manages to look on the positive side of things and it was just perfect when he reminded Fiona that this was what she wanted: a short labor to avoid having to take those antibiotics. This was just the sort of encouragement she needed at this difficult time. When I took her to the bathroom and she felt the urge to push with the next contraction while sitting on the toilet, I realized that we really were in for a short, sharp labor. A few contractions later and I suggested to Simon that he might phone the Birth Center. I must say, he sounded so very on top of things when he made his phone call – since he had been brilliant at timing not only the contractions, but also the duration of time between them (two minutes 15 seconds apart and lasting about one minute). Add to this the background noise of Fiona having a contraction, followed by Simon's comment, "Oh and she has the urge to push," and it was hardly surprising that Beatrice commanded him to "bring her in immediately!"

Fiona managed to get into the car and was driven off to the Birth Center by Simon at 2:20 pm. I followed in my car, as I didn't want Simon to have to drive me home again after the birth. By the time we reached the Birth Center Fiona was most definitely pushing with every contraction and this seemed to be a little easier on her than those earlier ones when she had been dilating very fast. She managed to straddle a chair for a while which seemed relatively comfortable, but was worried about soil-ing the chair. (Never have I met anyone so fastidious in such a late stage of labor before!) To our utter amazement, when Jenny the midwife finally came in to examine her at around 2:45 pm, she was found to be completely dilated and was told to keep on pushing to her heart's content. I think that this was probably another point for Fiona when her mind could barely keep up with her incredibly efficient body. "Push?" "Already??" "But I've only been in labor for a couple of hours! It's not supposed to be this fast with a first baby!" However, push she did with strength and vigor. There is nothing quite so magnificent as to witness a woman birthing her baby with all the power and energy that is involved. Fiona's supportive team was comprised of Simon, the midwives Tania and Jenny, and me. We were awestruck observers as we watched the birth process take over and lead Fiona through that last hour of labor as she worked to push her baby out. She herself instinctively found the optimal position on all fours and our job was simply to reassure and encourage her as she performed this momentous and miraculous task of birthing her baby. She even managed to stall the event while Simon drove home to fetch the cord blood kit. I had thought of offering to go but was worried about finding their house and the kit. Fiona just looked at me and said "I'll be able to wait for him," which is exactly what she did.

By 3:10 pm the baby's head was clearly visible and Simon was able to touch it. I will never forget the look of wonder on his face as his fingers made their first contact with his child's mop of thick black hair. Fiona was very brave and managed to push through the intense burning sensation of the crowning stage. At long last, there was her baby's head – half out, resting and waiting patiently for Mom's next contraction. Simon was able to hold the baby's head and I even managed to take a photo. We persuaded Fiona to reach down again and touch her baby's head for the second time. There was a wonderful feeling of patience and calm despite Fiona's amazing energy. Finally, at 3:21 pm the entire, perfect body of baby Rhiannon slipped out into the big wide world and into the capable hands of her Dad, who delivered her as if he had been doing it all his life.

I think it is safe to call this adorable little being Rhiannon, but I dare not venture as to whether or not she will have another name – and if so, what it will be. To date, the decision on what to name her has not yet been made. But no matter – there is plenty of time for such details.

Fiona was quite literally in shock as a result of the speed with which she had man-aged to bring this baby into the world and started shaking violently. Simon held his daughter in his arms as if he would never let her go. Jenny delivered the placenta, which was clearly a great relief to Fiona, and then had to give her just a few stitches for a small tear. Meanwhile, Simon was getting to know his new daughter in a quiet and dedicated way. Such strong bonding in the first few minutes. What a wonderful start in life – to be followed by a magnificent first feeding, which lasted most of the rest of the afternoon. Once she had latched on, she just wouldn't let go for hours! What more could a newborn wish for?

During the course of the rest of the afternoon, numerous visitors arrived. First Leslie, Simon's sister, who was so thrilled to meet her baby niece. She was then followed by an onslaught of aunts, uncles, cousins and friends. The joy and love in that room was palpable. I was worried that Fiona was going to get tired out, but her resilience seemed unending. She relished sharing all the details of the birth with every visitor and was clearly far too excited to be tired. She had every reason to be the proudest woman on earth that day.

Short, sharp labors are not easy labors. They are incredibly intense and difficult to keep up with, leaving the mother in a state of shock. At one point I told her that she was a very strong woman and doing brilliantly. She retorted, "You are paid to say that!" I have been cussed at, yelled at and even struck at by women in labor but no one has ever come out with that one before! But, I was being absolutely 100% honest when I said, "You are a strong woman."

Rhiannon had Apgars of 9 and 10, which shows how well she tolerated this short, sharp labor. When Tania finally got around to weighing her, she was 8 lbs. 10 oz. — more than any of us predicted. She was 20 inches long, her head measured 36 cm around and her chest 35½ cm. She was a perfect baby, as she exemplified by her laying for a couple of hours, content and totally relaxed, in her grandmother's arms after that very long first feeding.

Thank you Fiona and Simon for allowing me to be present at this wondrous birth. We traveled together on a rollercoaster journey today, which will remain in my heart forever. Your strength will be an inspiration to me in my work as a doula and will serve to constantly remind me how wonderful birth can be.

"Fiona reached the car and leaned over the front seat to deal with the next contraction."

CLARISSE'S BIRTH

I'm all for planning ahead. Anticipation and preparation, in fact, play a big part in my own personal "wiring." Couple this with my years of experience as a doula, and I must say I've become pretty adept at anticipating "the next thing," when it comes to the process of labor and childbirth. That said, I was completely caught off guard – along with everyone else – by the rapid arrival of little Clarisse.

Fiona's baby was due around August 18th and because I was to be out of town during that time, I introduced Fiona to Sonya as a back-up doula, in case of my absence. Little did we know that we would both miss the event! On Wednesday afternoon at 3:30 pm, Sonya and I had arranged to meet at the Fiona's home, in order to get acquainted (or in my case, reacquainted) with husband Simon and their fifteen month old daughter Rhiannon. I had the honor of being the doula at Rhiannon's birth the previous year. Fiona had been having irregular contractions for a few hours and had just lost her mucous plug. I was quick to inform her that in some cases this could happen days before labor really kicked in. I didn't want anyone assuming that this baby was going to be born within hours! *I was wrong!*

Fiona had two or three contractions while we were all chatting and playing on the floor with Rhiannon and the strongest one took her breath away and forced her to stop talking mid-sentence. I began to think that maybe this was early, early labor. *Wrong again!* Having made sure that they had all the necessary phone numbers, Sonya and I left just before 5:00 pm. I advised Fiona to rest a little, because if she was in early labor, she may have a sleepless night ahead of her and needed to nap before the long haul. As I was driving home I predicted delivery at around 2:00 am the next morning. *Wrong yet again!*

Simon and Rhiannon went out to run errands and left Fiona to take her nap. There was not much napping, however, as contractions grew in strength and frequency. At 6:00 pm, Fiona got on the phone with her friend Crissy to warn her that she may just have to take care of Rhiannon in the next day or two, as it seemed like her baby could be on the way. On the other hand, as Crissy pointed out, this could just as easily be a "false labor."

Shortly after 6:00 pm, Simon and Rhiannon arrived home and it was just as well, because Fiona's contractions were really building up. I think by now Fiona knew that she was truly in labor! She started to get her things together for the trip to the Birth Center, but had a lot of trouble finding her crampbark and other herbs which she was hoping might slow contractions down a bit. As she wandered around the house looking for her things, she had to lean on whatever was available every time a contraction came.

At 6:25 pm Simon phoned me to tell me that Fiona's contractions were coming hard and fast. Hearing a loud groan and a very obvious pushing sound in the background, I suggested he phone the Birth Center immediately. I told him that I would come to their house and if they weren't there, I'd go on to the Birth Center. Simon spoke to Beatrice and asked her to page Jenny, who was the midwife on call. How fortunate we were to have the exact same birth team as the last time (for Rhiannon's birth) – a wonderfully compassionate midwife and a caring, gentle nurse. Simon was told to bring Fiona in right away. As they started walking towards their Suburban which was parked in the garage, another huge contraction came with strong urges to push.

Fiona reached the car and leaned over the front seat to deal with the next contraction. As the contraction grew in force she felt her baby travel down the birth canal and the head appeared. The contraction continued with its full force and the rest of the baby was pushed out into the dark world of Fiona's maternity pants! Simon had tried to hold the baby in by supporting her head, but as he quickly realized, the powers of nature are beyond our control. At 6:40 pm, with gentle, loving hands, Simon held the baby from behind and drew her out into the open air. All this while, 15-month-old Rhiannon sat in her car seat watching her baby sister's strange entry into the world. In previous discussions, Simon had been adamant that he wanted to hold the baby as she was being delivered, but I don't think he had *"preventing her from falling down a dark trouser leg"* in mind when he said that!

As an inseparable threesome – Fiona holding Clarisse Marie with the cord still attached and Simon supporting them both – they all hobbled back to the house and dialed 911. The anonymous female voice on the other end of the phone gave Simon some impersonal but sensible instructions about tying a knot in the cord using a shoelace, along with, "don't listen to what your wife says." I'm not sure how sensible *that* bit of advice was! By the time the firemen eventually found their driveway, Fiona and Clarisse had painfully maneuvered themselves into the back of the Suburban and were ready to go to the Birth Center. Fiona recalls that the sight of nine muscular and uniformed firemen bearing down on her did not inspire any desire to be whisked off to the hospital in an ambulance. She steadfastly stayed put and convinced Simon to drive her to the Birth Center. Rhiannon found it all quite exciting and urged her daddy to "go faster" over the speed bumps – with every jostle crushing Fiona's bruised sacrum.

I arrived at the Birth Center at the same time as this new family of four. I'm the birth doula who is supposed to give continuous support during labor, not turn up *after* the baby is born! There in the front seat, Beatrice gave Clarisse some oxygen as she was turning a bit blue, and having cut the cord, immediately took her into the Birth Center. Then came more painful maneuvering for Fiona as she had to step gingerly out of the Suburban and make her own way inside the facility. Strong woman that she is, she refused the office chair Beatrice had brought for her and insisted on walking in. As she did so her placenta came out and we were thankful for those famous maternity pants being somewhat in place. (They should be framed for posterity.) Finally, she reached Clarisse's crib and leaned over to say her first real "hello" to her new daughter. As she did this, I heard Karen, a midwife, gently whisper to her, "We think she may have Down's Syndrome." I can't imagine what was going through Fiona's head at that moment, but for me the world literally stood still as I gazed into Clarisse's beautiful face.

It was going to be necessary to take Clarisse over to the Intensive Care Unit at the medical center, so it was decided that Simon should go with his daughter and Fiona would do her postpartum recovery at the Birth Center. By this time, Fiona's friend Crissy had arrived and was taking wonderful care of Rhiannon. The last I saw of Simon that day, was him being strapped onto the gurney clasping his little daughter. At that point, I knew the right thing was happening. Fiona needed time to absorb all the turmoil of the last few hours and to be cared for by her midwives and nurses. Simon was the right person to accompany his daughter – I just wish he had had the support of a doula, as it must have been a nerve-wracking night for him.

I tried to be there completely for Fiona during the next few hours as she traveled along a turbulent path of extreme emotions, from sadness to anger, from guilt to disbelief, from anguish to fear. Our midwife Jenny was a wonderful support and I shall always remember her saying, "It's normal and right to be feeling all these different emotions now. But deep down in the depths of your soul, you know, Fiona, that you did nothing wrong – that this is *not* your fault, that there *is* no reason."

Finally, in the early hours of the morning, Simon came to join us at the Birth Center. He decided to sleep for a few hours there with Fiona and Rhiannon while his mother stayed at the hospital with Clarisse. I left the three of them together, curled up on the bed. In the NICU, Clarisse's condition was stable and the prognosis was good. She was going to be fine.

It's going to be an exciting and challenging path finding a new and different way of life with Clarisse. She is a very lucky little girl to have been born into such a caring and compassionate family. As for me, I just wish I'd never left their house at 5:00 pm – but who could have guessed?

MY YOUNGEST
Daughter's
BIRTH

"As he moved up into second gear, he looked over and saw the baby's head emerge."

EURO-BÉBÉ: KATE

This is the story of Kate's birth at 5:00 pm on Monday, July 27, 1992 – a stone's throw away from the European Parliament in Strasbourg, France.

As a childbirth educator, I have been asked "At what point should we go into hospital when labor starts?" umpteen times over the years. Anxious fathers often ask for advice on emergency deliveries. I have always coolly added to my reply: "Don't worry, I don't know anybody who has actually had her baby in the supermarket or in the car." Well, now I do ....me.

I visited my obstetrician at 3:00 pm on Monday and he confirmed my suspicion that my waters were leaking slightly. He proceeded to fit me with a series of acupressure points: a dozen or so circular metal disks the size of a pin head which he attached to specific labor-stimulating locations on my body with sticky tape. They were carefully placed on my wrists, my ankles, and my legs. These pressure points, he assured me, would help things along given that I was already at 40 weeks and 1cm dilated. This is not common practice in France, but my doctor is one of a kind in Strasbourg, who believes in low-tech, mother-controlled labors. "Madame, you can have your baby hanging from the chandelier," he quipped one time when I was asking him about positions for labor. "Come and see me again in two days if nothing has happened and keep a careful check on your temperature to make sure that you have no infection," he said this time. "Call me immediately if you show any sign of fever."

I was having irregular contractions by this time and as a neighbor was looking after my two older children, Johanna and Alastair, and since we lived half an hour's drive from Strasbourg, I suggested to my husband, Rob, that we visit some friends in town for a cup of tea. This way we would only be 10 minutes drive from the clinic should I need to go there sooner rather than later. My French doctor was highly amused that his English patient was thinking about a cup of tea at such an exciting time.

The acupressure seemed to take instant effect and I knew I was really in labor before the tea was brewed. Rob kitted me out with a TENS unit which I had rented from England, because in France the choice of pain relief is epidural or nothing. TENS stands for Transcutaneous Electrical Nerve Stimulation, and consists of four stimulating pads placed on the back, which transmit mild electrical impulses through the skin and offer a tingling sensation as a distraction to the contractions. I found the TENS machine really helpful, along with Vivaldi's Stabat Mater on the Walkman and Rob's reassuring presence at my side. I rocked gently to the music, turning the TENS unit up to its maximum for each contraction and floated off into a labor trance.

When contractions became really powerful, after only one hour, I told myself that I must still have a long way to go. After all, only an hour had passed. Rob, however, took one look at me and insisted that it was time to leave. I remember believing that if I stood up and moved away from the rocking chair, I would be able to leave the contraction behind and escape from it's intensity. However, when I did actually stand up, I immediately felt the baby moving down low into my pelvis. I was incapable of conveying the immediacy of the situation to Rob who was desperately trying to drag me out of the front door towards the car. I was beyond speech, in a world of my own, my primeval instincts had completely taken over and I was birthing a baby. Later, he told me that I was groaning loudly on the way out to the car and beginning to make "powerful grunting noises!"

My waters broke after a couple of minutes in the car – fortunately, my ever prepared husband had several large, clean towels which he had placed under me on the front seat. By the time we reached the first red light, I could feel the baby's head with my hand. At the next set of lights, I began to rip my shorts off to incredulous looks from Rob. As he moved up into second gear, he looked over and saw the baby's head emerge. By the time he had pulled the car over and rushed round to the passenger's door, I was holding Kate in my arms, with a beatific and dazed look on my face. She had slipped out gently into my waiting arms and I had scooped her up and held her tightly to my belly.

We wrapped her in a large clean towel and set off again. At the next light, we spotted a friend, Bridget, who had just finished her working day at the Council of Europe. She was standing at the side of the road waiting for her husband to pick her up. She waved at us and sauntered over to say hello. Her expression changed from a casual smile to sheer stupefaction as she realized that I was sitting, half naked, in the front seat holding a newborn infant with the umbilical cord still attached. Without further ado, she hopped into the back seat and the four of us continued on to the clinic. Bridget did a marvelous job of checking Rob's potentially reckless driving in rush hour traffic, and it was Bridget who peeped and informed us that we had a daughter.

We had been too stunned to look at the baby's sex ourselves.

On arrival at the clinic 10 minutes later, Rob rushed in to fetch the midwife. She finally came out and cut the cord in the car, and Kate and I were taken up to the Labor and Delivery room where the only thing left to deliver was the placenta. It was a marvelous feeling to arrive at the clinic, having already finished the hard work. Rob gave Kate her first bath and I nursed her afterwards. When my doctor finally turned up on the scene to give me a couple of small repair stitches, his first question was: "Did you have time for a cup of the English tea?"

This whirlwind delivery was nothing like the calm, gentle birthing we had planned and expected at the clinic. Yet, it was such an empowering experience; I felt strong and invincible, capable of anything. I was so proud of myself and felt a new respect for my own strength and stamina. I will always feel gratitude towards my lovely daughter for being in such a hurry and giving me the opportunity to live this incredible adventure.

GLOSSARY

Acupressure: An element of traditional Chinese medicine which involves applying firm pressure to specific acupuncture points on the body, in order to release blocked energy and restore balance.

Amnio infusion: A saline solution is placed into the uterus to treat problems associated with decreased amniotic fluid volume.

Amniohook: Resembling a crochet hook, the amniohook is used to artificially rupture the bag of membranes.

Amniotic fluid: A watery fluid contained inside the amniotic sac (bag of water) in which the fetus resides.

Apgar score: A rating given to a newborn at one and five minutes after birth to assess skin color, heart rate, muscle tone, respiration and reflexes. Zero to 2 points are given for each category. Scores approaching 10 are considered healthy.

Birth Center: Family-centered care where women can give birth in a safe, home-like environment with qualified midwives who practice a wellness and holistic approach to pregnancy, birth, and women's health care.

Bloody show: Blood-tinged mucous from the vagina, also known as the mucous plug, discharged before and/or during labor.

Breech position: When the baby is positioned with feet or bottom toward the cervix at the time of birth.

Catheter: A tube that is inserted through the urethra into the bladder to drain urine. Frequently used for women who have an epidural.

Cervidil: Prostaglandin vaginal insert used to prepare the cervix for induction of labor.

Cervix: The neck-like lower part of the uterus, which dilates and thins during labor to allow for passage of the baby.

GLOSSARY

Cesarean: Surgery performed in which an incision is made through the abdominal wall and uterus to deliver the baby.

Cord blood: The blood that is in the placenta and umbilical cord which contains stem cells that can be used for treating genetic disorders.

Crampbark: An herbal remedy that helps ease spasmodic muscle contractions. It is sometimes used for painful menstrual cramps and to slow down an early or intense labor.

Cytotec: A medication approved by the FDA to treat ulcers, this medication is also used to ripen the cervix and induce labor.

Decels: Decelerations, referring to the fetal heart rate during labor.

Dilation: Indicates the diameter of the cervical opening and is measured in centimeters from 0 – 10 centimeters which is considered full dilation.

Down's syndrome: A chromosomal disorder caused by the existence of an extra chromosome.

Effacement: The thinning of the cervix during late pregnancy and labor, measured from 0 – 100%, which is considered fully effaced.

Episiotomy: A surgical incision in the perineum to enlarge the vaginal opening for passage of the baby.

Fore water: Part of the bag of waters trapped between the baby's head and the cervix when the baby engages in the pelvis

Group B Streptococcus (GBS): A bacterium commonly found in the flora of the female genital tract which can cause severe infections in newborns if it is passed to the baby during birth.

Heplock: A heparin lock. Heplocks also known as saline locks are IV's that are not connected to tubing. Should an emergency arise, the IV is already in place for immediate use.

Hind water: Part of the bag of waters behind the baby's head, closer to her body.

Hoku point: An acupressure point on the back of the hand on the webbing between the thumb and the index finger. It may speed up a slow-to-start labor and/or ease the pain of contractions.

Hypnobirthing: A form of childbirth preparation in which the woman learns how to relax deeply during her pregnancy and recalls this state of deep relaxation during labor.

IV: Intravenous drip giving liquid substances directly into a vein.

Meconium: The product of a baby's first bowel movement, green in color. Passing meconium in the uterus may be a sign of fetal distress.

Nipple stimulation: A way of bringing on or speeding up labor due to the release of the hormone oxytocin, which causes contractions.

OB: Obstetrician.

Oxytocin: A hormone, produced in the pituitary gland that causes contractions. It is also known as the bonding or cuddle hormone and the hormone of love.

Placental abruption: Separation of the placenta from the inner wall of the uterus before delivery.

Pessary: A vaginal suppository.

Phenergan: A medication used to relieve the symptoms of allergic reactions.

GLOSSARY

Pitocin: The synthetic form of the hormone oxytocin, commonly used to induce labor.

Placenta: The circular, flat organ that is responsible for oxygen, nutrients and waste products traveling from mother to baby in utero. The placenta leaves the uterus after the baby is born.

Prostaglandin gel: A medication that is used to soften the cervix and induce the onset of labor.

RN: Registered nurse.

Spinal Block: An anesthetic technique in which medication is injected into the fluid surrounding the spinal nerves resulting in anesthesia in a segment of the body.

Spleen 6 point: An acupressure point on the inner side of the lower leg, about four fingerbreadths above the ankle. It may help stimulate a slow-to-start labor.

Stadol: A morphine type analgesic used to relax women during labor and ease the sensations of contractions.

Station: A measurement of the descent of a fetus in the pelvis, measured in centimeters from -4 through 0 to +4.

Suture: Stitches performed during an episiotomy or a cesarean.

Telemetry: Allows the laboring woman to be remotely connected to the monitoring machine and not attached to it by wires.

TENS: Transcutaneous Electrical Nerve Stimulation, a hand held battery operated device which transits mild electrical impulses through the skin to stimulate nerve fibers in the back. It reduces pain in labor while allowing the woman freedom to walk and is commonly used in maternity wards in Canada, Australia and the UK.

Ultrasound: Using high frequency sound waves to view the fetus in the uterus.

Vacuum extractor: A tool with a rubber or plastic cup that can be attached to the baby's head, providing suction and aiding in delivery.

VBAC: Vaginal Birth After Cesarean.

Vernix: A slippery, white waterproof substance covering the skin of the fetus.

This glossary is designed to give a brief description of the technical terms used in the stories. It is no way a substitute for medical advice. If you have any questions about your pregnancy, birth or newborn, please consult your midwife or doctor.

Penny Bussell Stansfield

Penny Bussell Stansfield was born and educated in the UK. She lived in France for 15 years before moving to the United States in 1995. Penny has been a childbirth educator in the UK, France and the US for 25 years. She became a DONA International Certified Birth Doula in 1997 and has attended over 100 births. In 1998, she was certified as a DONA International Birth Doula Trainer and has taught more than 30 workshops nationwide.

In 2000, Penny became a licensed massage therapist, with a specialization in working with pregnant women. She is one of the creators of the Cortiva Institute's Maternity and Infant Massage Program, a graduate-level course for certified massage therapists taught throughout the US. Penny is currently the co-owner of Hillsborough Massage Therapy LLC in Hillsborough, NJ where she specializes in prenatal and postpartum massage. She is also on the education team at Mama Mio Ltd., an international provider of safe and effective high-quality skincare products for pregnancy and postpartum.

Penny understands that the birthing experience is a transformative event in a woman's life. Her professional activities are focused on nurturing women through touch, emotional support and education during pregnancy, birth and postpartum.

She lives with her husband Rob in New Jersey and has three children.

Please visit *www.pennydoula.com*.

KATE STANSFIELD, right (pictured below), with her brother and sister, Alastair and Johanna.

PENNY WITH HER doula babies and their moms (above). Penny with her doula babies (left).